The Hand for Spelling Dictionary

The Hand for Spelling Dictionary

Charles Cripps
Margaret Peters

Illustrated by Bryony Jacklin

The Hand for Spelling Dictionary
Ref.LD 983
ISBN 1 85503 109 4
© Charles Cripps, Margaret Peters
© Illustrations Bryony Jacklin
All rights reserved
First published 1991

LDA, Duke Street, Wisbech, Cambs PE13 2AE

Printed in Great Britain by
Ebenezer Baylis & Son Ltd
The Trinity Press, Worcester, and London

Introduction

The Hand for Spelling Dictionary is a collection or bank of words used by children in their writing. It is designed as a store of words that children in the 7–11 age range seem most likely to use in the course of their free writing. Nevertheless, the list is not limited to use by this age group. Since its aim is primarily to help individuals who can read but have difficulty with their spelling, it can also be used by older children or adults who need help in this area.

By dictionary definition, a 'bank' is not only a place of custody but also a place which can be counted upon; which can be reckoned as reliable. *The Hand for Spelling Dictionary* is a word bank which can be counted upon to provide children with the words they need. It is also more than a bank because highlighted in every word it contains is a letter string which children need to be familiar with before they can attempt, in their own writing, words they have never written before. In addition, anyone looking up a word also receives a 'bonus' by seeing a group of other words with the same letter string.

A child wanting a word looks it up, using dictionary techniques, and learns the word by looking at it, covering it and writing it down from memory. Attention is then given to the 'bonus' words in the columns on the right of this stimulus word, since these contain the same letter string. They are there to start the child on the path to generalisation of letter strings – an ability essential to good spelling.

The technique used in *The Hand for Spelling Dictionary* is entirely visual. There is no auditory strategy whatever, other than reading the word. This is because as soon as a word is broken up or sounded out, the way is open to indecision. For example, a child wants to write the word 'daughter'. If it is sounded, the child would start with 'd . . . or? aw?', and thus the child might easily write 'dortur', 'dawtir' or any of the many alternative spellings possible if speech sounds are used instead of letter strings. But if the child thinks of 'daught' as in 'caught' and 'laughter' (in other words is aware of visual similarity), the child is more likely to make a reasonable attempt, even though it may not be a completely accurate version of the word 'daughter'.

1

Auditory, phonic or phonetic strategies can be extremely precarious ways into learning to spell. In learning words from *The Hand for Spelling Dictionary* the child is using an entirely visual strategy. It is important, therefore, to consider what this implies.

Spelling by Looking

There is evidence that being able to spell depends more than anything on looking at words in a very special way. As adults, what do *we* do if we do not know how to spell a word? We write it down to see if it looks right.

Vision is our preferred sense, so we check visually. It is, therefore, crucial that we look at that part of the word which is likely to give trouble. There is evidence that children do not do this. For example, in a study of eye movements, Gilbert (1932) described an efficient 12-year-old speller, who in the pre-test wrote 'definitely' as 'definitly'. In the subsequent learning of its spelling, her eye movement record showed that she paid very little attention to the 'e' which she had previously omitted. Another 12-year-old, in learning to spell the word 'questionnaire', spent most of the learning period on the study of the word 'question', which she had spelled correctly in the pre-test. In spite of 'knowing' the word, she studied it.

The Hand for Spelling Dictionary highlights the letter strings within words that may cause trouble. It also highlights words containing the same letter string; words that children may already know, and will undoubtedly need.

The book is a store of selected words which, it has been found, children want to write. They learn these – not by copying but by a kind of imaging of whole words. (For further discussion about the importance of developing this 'kind of imagery' see Peters (1985) pages 48–51.) The words to which the children refer in the basic list direct them to other, similarly constructed words which they read peripherally – and connect on the basis of common letter strings. These are bonus words which they may or may not already be able to spell.

It does not matter if the child does not actually learn these words. The important bit of learning is the learning of the letter string, and above all the fact that letter strings recur, often in the most unlikely words; for example, **eigh** in n**eigh**bour or **ome** in w**ome**n. It is through this visual referencing that children begin generalising from the spelling system.

Any words that children need to write must be learnt at the time the words are needed. In order to do this they must follow a routine which will prevent them from copying without thinking. It is vital, therefore, that children are taught a reliable and psychologically sound way of learning to spell, and that is by attending to the word structure, with the firm purpose of reproducing the word they want without copying.

The teacher must insist on the following routine:

1 LOOK at the word carefully and in such a way that you will remember what you have seen.

2 COVER the word so that you cannot see it.

3 WRITE the word in your book from memory, saying it softly to yourself as you are writing.

4 CHECK what you have written. If you have not written the word correctly, do not alter it, but go back and repeat all these steps.

Spelling by Writing

Writing, like talking, is an expressive skill that is vital for children to acquire. Parents are worried if their children fail to learn to talk. They are delighted when they do talk. They are equally delighted when they see them writing, when they see them 'spinning something out of their own head'; for here is something that they are generating for themselves.

Furthermore, the main reason for learning to spell is to be able to write accurately. Rarely in adult life do we spell out a word orally. So it is in writing that children learn to spell. This is the motor side of a *visuo-motor* (hand/eye) activity. It is a visual ability which is 'firmly cemented in writing' (Schonell, 1942).

There is also a very close connection between well-ordered and consistent writing and good spelling, for children who develop a confident and flowing joined writing style from the beginning and also study the structure of words are released to concentrate on the content of their writing (Cripps and Cox, 1989).

Spelling Lists

The teaching of spelling needs to be approached in a positive and systematic manner. In some schools, however, if spelling is taught at all, teachers believe that it must be taught through spelling lists. If teachers are making this assumption, then it is appropriate to examine the whole concept of lists.

Undoubtedly, the words children use in their own writing will provide the teacher with an extremely sound basis on which to construct lists. Certainly, teachers are fully aware that the most useful spelling vocabulary is that supplied by children themselves in the course of their own free writing. Therefore, before using a published list, the discerning teacher would want to know to what extent such a list was based on either children's spoken or written language. Unfortunately, many spelling lists have been derived from adults' writing and reading material, and children have been expected to learn these words, rather than those from their own writing needs.

On the other hand, if lists are derived from words which the children ask for in the course of their writing, or words which relate to those they ask for, there 'is significantly greater progress than from printed lists or no lists at all' (Peters, 1970). Teachers who use printed lists tend to rely entirely on these to teach children to spell. The children learn a list each day, often in a way they have worked out for themselves and one that is unsatisfactory. These words are subsequently tested, again by some arbitrary and often unsound method. Indeed, in mixed ability classes the words in a printed list are unlikely to be suitable for the whole range within the class.

Although the National Curriculum has set out quite clearly the statements of attainment, it is very unlikely that these will be met by using published lists. Few offer teaching strategies to offset the haphazard and uneconomic techniques which children evolve if left to themselves. If children are given a list to learn, they may spell out the word alphabetically by letter names (a traditional but time-consuming method) or they may copy the word letter by letter, rather than taking in the whole word and writing it from memory. So often we see children making letter by letter associations; looking at one letter – writing it, looking at the next letter – writing it. Such a strategy is obviously a psychologically unsound way into spelling. Letters by themselves do not represent particular sounds. Only when letters are within an environment of other letters do they represent particular sounds. That is why it is letter strings, not single letters, that matter, and these must be learned.

Sometimes by common sense, or by chance, some children hit on strategies of their own, dependent on associative learning techniques or mnemonics. These children are fortunate, but it is unwise to leave the finding of a strategy for learning such a basic tool to chance.

What The Hand for Spelling Dictionary provides:

- A learning strategy for the actual word the child wishes to write.
- A means of generalisation to other words which have the same internal structure.
- A collection of words which it has been found that children in the 7–11 age range want to write.

A learning strategy

Strategies and generalisation like this are visuo-motor, that is, they depend on eye and hand. Entries in *The Hand for Spelling Dictionary* are, therefore, accompanied by lists of words of similar structure. The aim is to teach children to make visual associations. For example, it is easy to associate 'cough' with 'tough' visually and easy to spell the word when the association has been made. But it is very difficult to spell 'cough' if the writer is relying on the way it sounds or on alphabetic recitation. Obviously children will not

4

learn to spell by merely looking and this awareness of visual structure must be cemented in writing. This is the motor aspect of the visuo-motor emphasis which is the principle on which this book is designed.

Generalisation

Here we are talking about generalisation to other words which have the same internal structure. On the whole children do not generalise unless they have been taught to perceive likenesses within words. They must be told by the teacher explicitly:

- These words look the same. For example, *horse* and *worse*.
- Look for the letter string that is the same. Or think about whether the word is like any other word.

They must be told to look carefully at a word and particularly at the highlighted letter string – which is likely to be the 'hard spot' – and then look at it in the other words in either the first or second column. These they will not actually learn by writing, but by relating letter strings. They will acquire the secret of spelling by generalisations rather than the tedious method of learning rules. For rule-learning and generalisation from rules rather than from letter strings depend upon a developmental level of mental operation that is often beyond many children.

A collection of words

Children want to write so that what is written can be read. The content is important but children must be able to spell adequately for other people to be able to read what has been written. So they must have access to the correct spelling of the words they want to use. Many of these are in this book. Those that are not must be asked for and the parent or teacher may then write them in their own personal word bank. From this the children will acquire a repertoire of words which they can use from their own vocabulary in their own idiom.

Design of The Hand for Spelling Dictionary

The Hand for Spelling Dictionary contains over 3000 words taken from:

- Alphabetical Spelling List, Levels 1 to 5 (1963).
- Key Words to Literacy, (1965).
- Word for Word, (1989).
- Incidental words selected because of their structural similarity to words in the above lists.

Some common words of three or four letters are omitted because their phonic regularity makes them relatively easy to write. The resulting list of 'stimulus' words is in alphabetical order. The bonus words are grouped on the basis of similarity of visual structure, that is, the principle for grouping is a letter string. For example, 'could' is grouped with 'would', 'should', 'shoulder', boulder etc. The rationale for this organisation is that spelling is predominantly a visual skill and therefore the auditory structure is of limited value. Obviously, some groups of bonus words will nevertheless have in them only words with both visual and auditory correspondence, for example, 'drift', 'lift' and 'gift'.

The words are listed across the page in three columns.

- The first column contains the *stimulus* word. For convenience these are in alphabetical order with the appropriate letter string highlighted. Because some words have more than one significant letter string they may appear more than once in the alphabetical list. For example, 'work' appears with letter strings 'ork' and also 'wor' highlighted. Obviously, the linking of letter strings across the words is endless and at times the cross-referencing or repetition of stimulus words may seem excessive. The purpose of this, however, is to provide as many different ways as possible to help children make meaningful visual associations. On the other hand, it will also be noted that some of the words in Level 2 may only appear once or twice in the first column. To highlight all possible letter strings would be excessive and only the most significant letter strings have been highlighted.

- The second column (Level 1) contains words from the known writing vocabularies of children in the 7–9 age range. All these words have the same letter string as the stimulus word. For example, 'cost' is with 'lost', 'frost', 'post' etc. In terms of reading, the teaching of phonic generalisation usually facilitates phonological awareness, hence the first word/words in this column usually demonstrate the same auditory and visual structure. They are then followed by other group/groups which will have a different auditory structure while containing the same letter string. Within each of these sub-groups the words are arranged in alphabetical order. The only exceptions to this ordering are the days of the week, months of the year and the numerals.

- The third column (Level 2) contains words from the known writing vocabularies of children in the 9–11 age range. Again all these words have the same letter string as the stimulus word and are arranged as in Level 1.

The words in the dictionary are all cross-referenced, that is, words from columns two and three are all included as stimulus words in the alphabetically-ordered first column. There are occasions when bonus words containing the same letter string appear in both columns; for example, the letter string 'age' appears in Level 1 in 'cage', 'page', 'rage' etc., and in

6

Level 2 in 'advantage', 'average' etc. The same bonus word, however, does not appear in both levels.

It is not intended that the words included in *The Hand for Spelling Dictionary* should be an exhaustive list. They form a base to which the teacher can make appropriate additions or deletions. Where there are blank spaces it is because there are no other words within that level containing the same letter string. It is here that the teacher is free to add words, preferably from the children's free writing. For example, 'leopard' could be listed with 'people' because of the letter string 'eop'.

How to Use The Hand for Spelling Dictionary

The Hand for Spelling Dictionary is primarily intended for children whose reading skills are developing adequately but who have remained poor spellers. When a child wishes to write a word and is uncertain of its spelling, the child looks down the first column which is alphabetically ordered. Obviously, this presupposes knowledge of dictionary techniques. The child finds the word, and by using reading ability is able to recognise it, though as yet, by definition, unable to reproduce it correctly. The child is then instructed to look at the highlighted letter string and then at the words to the right. All these words contain the same letter string, which has been highlighted, in the stimulus word. Of course the words may sound different. *This does not matter.* They are connected by visual reference only, for example, 'done', 'none', 'gone', 'bone' etc.

The child then reads the words but does not necessarily write them down. By reading and looking at the words attentively the child will note the internal letter string. Possibly one of the words in the group may already be known and this will consolidate the spelling of the stimulus word.

This reading of the bonus word is not the kind of reading children employ in the normal course of reading from a book, since these words are divorced from context and therefore the child is unable to draw from any other psycho-linguistic cues (in other words from the kind of redundancies that help us along the line and down the page). The child is looking, with interest, intent and intention to recall, at word structure.

The success of the transfer that occurs depends on the child's ability to recognise similar visual structures – and these are highlighted in the text. This reading of the bonus words must be low key, without heavy instruction and anxiety. It is peripheral.

Inherent in the whole idea of *The Hand for Spelling Dictionary* is the autonomy of the teacher no less than that of the child. Teachers must use the book as they see fit. It is 'safe' however it is used, because it is dependent on visual imagery and attention to letter strings. The child's own writing will stimulate the use of it, and the teacher is able to relate the words and show the child how to relate the word to other similarly constructed words. Nevertheless, the degree of success will undoubtedly depend on how carefully the children are taught to use the *The Hand for Spelling Dictionary* and the quality of the dictionary instruction by the teacher in the matter of good spelling habits.

Although the main function of *The Hand for Spelling Dictionary* is as a reference book of words needed for writing, it also has other functions:

- Children who find reading difficult still want to write, and writing can indeed aid the development of literacy. For such children *The Hand for Spelling Dictionary* can spark off the realisation that words are made up of 'strings' of letters – a realisation that makes English orthography not such a frightening medium after all.

- For older children or adults who can read and find spelling difficult, *The Hand for Spelling Dictionary* is a less formidable and more independent way into spelling than the conventional dictionary. Moreover, it emphasises letter cohesion, and this is only another way of saying that they are learning about sequences or 'serial probability', which is what spelling is all about.

- For some individual children *The Hand for Spelling Dictionary* can be used solely as an alphabetically-ordered list. If the structurally similar words are presented at the same time, the cross-referencing system provides an opportunity for repetition and writing practice.

It is crucial that teachers are alerted to the dangers of feeling inhibited and constrained by such an organised word list. They must, instead, be encouraged to experiment and innovate in terms of presentation and method. The important principle, is, when teaching the words, to ensure that children look at the words with an intention to reproduce them – and then write them without copying. This must be the starting point of any spelling teaching.

The Role of the Teacher

It is indisputable that there is no one approach to the teaching of reading. This is equally true of spelling. This, then, is the case for *The Hand for Spelling Dictionary*, a resource which is individual, and open-ended. Most important of all, it challenges the sensitive teacher to exploit children's linguistic resources so that they can write as easily as they can speak.

Interest in words

To achieve this the teacher must capture children's interest in words since children can learn more successfully if they are curious about language.

Interest in word structure

In addition to being captivated by the interplay of words, semantically and syntactically, they must also become intrigued by the way words are composed in particular kinds of patterns. They will then see a word like 'fernipendity' as acceptable whereas 'sgikmraqutut' is not. Again this depends on letter strings that fit acceptably into words that children are learning. This is why sets of words like 'above', 'glove', 'love' and 'lovely' must be grouped with 'move', 'prove', 'drove' and 'stove'. Such words are being grouped according to the way they look rather than the way they sound.

Obviously, some children are unlikely to remember all the peripheral and bonus words. They will, however, have had the opportunity of seeing them and associating them with a similar word which they already know. The teacher's task, then, is to point out the visual similarities and differences between words. Probably even more important than such arbitrary associations are spelling patterns that are lexically related; for example, 'sign' and 'signal'. But these must be pointed out. The more lexically related words children know and find for themselves, the more they will search for them. They will find that 'nation' will connect with 'national' or 'story' with 'history' and then with 'historical'.

Increasing the span of apprehension

There is considerable evidence that it is not visual acuity but the *way* we look at words that makes for good spelling. It is learning to increase the *amount* which we can take in at a glance and reproduce in writing, that is crucial. That is why it is important to train children in visual imagery. They are told to look at a word and then to visualise it on a blank wall, or finger trace it on the table, or, as one teacher put it, 'see it on the inside of your eyelids'.

The Look-Cover-Write-Check routine may begin with short words or even parts of words, but the *increase* of the amount that can be taken in at one eyeful as it were (the span of apprehension) is vital, and the teacher can demand longer words or sequences of words to be looked at, visualised and reproduced from memory.

Obviously, some words will contain 'hard spots' and these must be identified by the teacher and related to other letter strings in words already known to the children.

Acquiring swift and consistently formed handwriting

It is not only for aesthetic reasons or legibility that handwriting is important. There is evidence to suggest that the careful writer tends to be the swift writer and speed of writing influences spelling ability (Peters, 1970). This implies the need for certainty of letter shapes where the writer is producing some form of 'running writing' with the letters in a continuous flow. This allows the writer to concentrate on the letter string and word structure rather than on the letter formation. In other words, children with swift motor control write groups of letters (for example, 'ough') in a connected form.

Acquiring a strategy for learning new words

Strategies for learning anything are, of course, individual. We all learn things in our own way. But in learning a skill which is ultimately a motor habit, as in the actual process of writing, some ways of learning are psychologically more sound than others.

The Look-Cover-Write-Check routine, which is fully endorsed in the National Curriculum, is a well-tried strategy emphasising looking, visualising and writing in learning to spell. In other words, the child is trained to look carefully at the structure of the word, endeavour to memorise it and then make an attempt to reproduce the whole word. If, after checking, the attempt is found to be incorrect then the procedure is repeated. This technique also helps to prevent letter by letter copying, which is psychologically unacceptable. Moreover, when teaching spelling there is always the problem of testing. *The Hand for Spelling Dictionary*, with the Look-Cover-Write-Check routine, ensures that children correct themselves and self-correction is the most productive form of correction.

The introduction of a multi-sensory approach, as advocated by Fernald

This technique, invaluable as a method for children with specific spelling difficulties, incorporates visual, auditory, tactile and kinaesthetic means of learning a new word.

The constant tracing and saying of a word encourages the children towards a global knowledge of the letter string and structure, thus leading to improved assimilation and retention.

But, as always it is to the teacher that we return; for it is through the teaching of visually associative strategies that children will learn to write as freely and adventurously as they can speak.

Finally, the explicit aim of *The Hand for Spelling Dictionary* is to make children independent in their writing by being autonomous in their learning strategies. In addition it is intended that this book will encourage teachers to reappraise their own techniques for teaching spelling. This in itself is a bonus, for, if teachers become intrigued by words and word structure, then children too will be infected by this interest. After all, words are the coinage we are giving children and the managing of this coinage is something in which we hope they, too, will delight. Indeed it is through enjoyment of words that children's creative writing is enhanced.

List of References

Alphabet Spelling List, New Zealand Council for Educational Research, 1963.

Cripps, C. and Cox, R. *Joining the ABC*, LDA, 1989.

Fernald, G.M. *Remedial Techniques in Basic School Subjects*, McGraw-Hill, 1943.

Gilbert, L.C. 'An experimental investigation of eye movements to spell words', *Psychological Monograph* X1iii, 3, 1932.

McNally, J. and Murray, M. *Key Words to Literacy*, School Master Publishing Company, 1965.

Peters, M.L. *Success in Spelling*, Cambridge Institute of Education, 1970.

Peters, M.L. *Spelling: Caught or Taught – A New Look*, Routledge and Kegan Paul, 1985.

Reid, D. *Word for Word*, LDA, 1989.

Schonell, F.J. *Backwardness in the Basic Subjects*, Oliver and Boyd, 1942.

able	table valuable vegetable
a**board**	board cupboard
ab**out**	out scout shout route
ab**ove**	glove love lovely move prove drove stove
abs**ence**	
ab**sent**	sent sentence present
acci**dent**	dental dentist
account	
acc**ount**	
accountant	
acc**ount**ant	
accoun**tant**	
account**ant**	
ache	
ach**ieve**	
ac**qua**inted	
acqu**ain**ted	
a**cross**	cross crossing
act	practice practise action
action	act practice practise
add	addition address ladder

12

independence silence

accountant

accountant fountain mountainous

account

account fountain mountainous

distant

distant vacant lantern advantage plantation quantity meant

preacher reaches

thieves

equal quality quantity quarrel

brain explain gain remain sprain

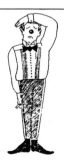

addition	add address ladder
ad dress	dress
address	add addition ladder
adopt	
adopted	
ad van tage	
advant age	
adv antage	
adven ture	
ad ven ture	
adv ice	
aerodrome	aeroplane
aeroplane	aerodrome
af ford	
aff ord	
af raid	raid
afr aid	laid maid paid raid said
aft	
aft er	afternoon aircraft

S. Pend,
57, Bend Road,
Mile End.

14

adopted

adopt

caravan van

average carriage courage damage postage sausage voyage

accountant distant vacant lantern plantation quantity meant

agriculture furniture future manufacture moisture nature temperature

event invent invention inventor prevent vent eleventh seventeen seventh

ice iceberg price spice notice service

ford

border cord ford record recorder

afterwards raft

afternoon	after aircraft
afterwards	
after**wards**	
afterw**ard**s	
again	against
ag**ain**	chain main pain paint plain
against	again
age	cage page rage stage bandage cabbage cottage language manage message village
ago	dragon
agree	
a**gree**	
agreement	
a**gree**ment	
agree**ment**	

agre**eme**nt	
agricul**ture**	
agric**ult**ure	
a**head**	headteacher

aft raft

backwards forwards towards

backwards forwards orchard towards cardboard guard harden pardon regard

agreement

agreement degree greeting

agree

agree degree greeting

amusement appointment argument development disappointment entertainment equipment improvement instrument ointment payment refreshment settlement statement

amusement improvement settlement statement extremely

adventure furniture future manufacture moisture nature temperature

difficult multiplication result

ahead	dead head instead bead lead leader
aim	claim
air	aircraft airport chair dairy fair fairly fairy hair pair
aircraft	after afternoon
air craft	air airport chair dairy fair fairly fairy hair pair
air port	air aircraft chair dairy fair fairly fairy hair pair
airport	important port report sport
alarm	arm army farm farmer harm warm
alike	
alive	
all	call hall small gallon shall valley allow (all right)
all ow	all call hall small gallon shall valley (all right)
all right	bright fright right
almost	most
almost	ghost most post cost frost lost
alone	bone telephone throne done none honey money one gone
along	belong long
along	belong long strong among
aloud	cloud loud
aloud	cloud loud proud

strike

attractive expensive forgive motive native deliver

al**read**y	bread ready spread thread read
al**so**	else
al**though**	though cough enough rough tough plough
alt hough	altogether salt
al**together**	together
altog**ether**	together whether
al**way** s	anyway away
am**ong**	along belong long strong
am**ount**	count country mount mountain

amuse

amuse

amuse ment

amuse**ment**

am**use** ment

amuseme nt

anc**ient**

anc ient

ang el

ang er

amusement

amusement fuse muse refuse

amuse

agreement appointment argument development
disappointment entertainment equipment improvement
instrument ointment payment refreshment settlement
statement

amuse fuse muse refuse

agreement improvement settlement statement extremely

scientist

fancy

anger exchange

angel exchange

anger	
angry	hungry
ank le	bank blanket drank
another	brother mother other bother
answer	
ant	pant plant elephant giant infants want
ants	infants
anxious	
any	many anybody anyhow anyone anything anywhere
any body	anyhow anyone anything anyway anywhere
anybody	body everybody nobody somebody
any how	many anybody anyone anything anyway anywhere
anyhow	how however somehow show
any one	many anybody anyhow anything anyway anywhere
anyone	everyone one someone
any thing	many anybody anyhow anyone anyway anywhere
anything	everything nothing something thing
any way	many anybody anyhow anyone anything anywhere
anyway	always away
any where	many anybody anyhow anyone anything anyway

dangerous stranger

delicious serious various

any**where**

a**part**

ape

appear

ap**pear**

appearance

ap**pear**ance

appear**ance**

apple

appoint

app**oint**

appointment

app**oint**ment

appoint**ment**

appreciate

appreci**at**e

appreci**ate**

appreciation

---

everywhere **no**where **some**where **where**

---

part parties party

---

happen

cape gape shape tape

appearance disappear disappearance

appearance disappear disappearance spear pear

appear disappear disappearance

appear disappear disappearance spear pear

disappearance importance instance nuisance

appointment disappoint disappointment

appointment disappoint disappointment ointment

appoint disappoint disappointment

appoint disappoint disappointment ointment

agreement amusement argument development disappointment entertainment equipment improvement instrument ointment payment refreshment settlement statement

appreciation

appreciation immediately

decorate skate state statement chocolate immediately pirate private whatever

appreciate

appreci **ation**

apprec **iation**

apricot

April

apron

are

area

aren't

argue

ar **gue**

argument

argu **ment**

are	aren't area square
aren't	are area square

arg **ument**

arm

army

a **round**

ar **ound**

ar **rest**

arm	alarm army farm farmer harm warm
army	alarm arm farm farmer harm warm
a **round**	ground playground round
ar **ound**	bound found ground mound playground pound round sound wound
ar **rest**	forest interested rest

association destination formation information irrigation multiplication occupation operation plantation recreation stationary stationery

appreciate immediately

April apron

apricot apron

apricot April

bare barely dare prepare rare share spare

argument

league tongue

argue

agreement amusement appointment development disappointment entertainment equipment improvement instrument ointment payment refreshment settlement statement

costume instrument

arr**ive**	dive drive driver five knives wives give live river
arrow	narrow
art	article smart quarter
article	art smart quarter
artist	
art**ist**	
ash	
ashamed	
ashamed	
ashore	
ash**ore**	
a**side**	
as**ide**	
ask	asking basket
asking	ask basket
a**sk**ing	skin
as**king**	baking king kingdom making taking
a**sleep**	sleep sleepy
ass	
assembly	lass class glass grass

cart chart particular partner tart

blister distant district minister mistake mistress scientist wrist listening

crash flash lash splash ashamed ashore

ash ashore crash flash lash splash

flame frame lame tame camera

ash ashamed crash flash lash splash

core explore fore ore score therefore tore wore forever foreign

consider

guide provide stride tide consider embroidery

passenger association brass pass

association

associ**ation**

---

ate   date gate hate late mate plate

---

atom

atom

atomic

atomic

at**tack**

att**ack**

at**tend**

att**end**

---

at**tent**ion   tent

attract**ive**

attr**act**ive

August

---

aunt   auntie haunt

aunt   auntie autumn haunt

---

auntie   aunt haunt

auntie   aunt autumn haunt

---

ass passenger brass pass

appreciation destination formation information irrigation multiplication occupation operation plantation recreation stationary stationery

atomic

atomic tomato tomatoes potato

atom

atom tomato tomatoes potato

stack tack

backwards crack jacket lack stack tack

pretend tender

calendar friendship independence independent pretend splendid tender

deliver expensive forgive motive native alive

exactly manufacture subtract tract subtraction traction character

author haul saucepan sausage

author	
autumn	aunt auntie haunt
ave**nue**	
aven**ue**	
avenue	
ave**rage**	
aver**age**	
average	
a**wake**	
awake	
a**way**	always anyway
aw**ful**	beautiful careful cheerful thankful wonderful
awh**ile**	mile pile while
a**while**	while
a**woke**	woke
a**woke**	broke smoke spoke woke
axe	

August haul saucepan sausage

continue

continue due rescue statue Tuesday value

average traveller grave slave

courage

advantage carriage courage damage postage sausage voyage

avenue traveller grave slave

mistake bakery

crawl hawk lawyer

tax

baby	babies probably
babies	baby probably
back	black pack quack sack track
backwards	
backwards	
backwards	
bacon	
badge	
bag	cabbage
bait	wait
bake	baker
bake	baker brake cake lake make rake shake snake take wake
baker	bake
baker	bake brake cake lake make rake shake snake take wake
bakery	
bakery	
baking	asking king kingdom making taking
balance	distance entrance chance dance
ball	football snowball balloon

afterwards forwards towards

attack crack jacket lack stack tack

afterwards forwards orchard towards cardboard guard harden pardon regard

judge knowledge ledge

awake mistake

celery discovery embroidery jewellery machinery mystery slippery stationery

balloon	ball football snowball
banana	
band	bandage husband
bandage	band husband
bandage	candle grand hand handkerchief handle sandals standard
band**age**	cabbage cottage language manage message village age cage page rage stage
b**ang**	hang rang sang
b**ank**	ankle blanket drank
b**are**	
b**are**ly	
ba**rely**	
b**ark**	dark mark market park
barred	
barrel	
b**arrier**	carrier
barrow	
ba**rrow**	
b**ase**	case chase
b**ask**et	ask asking
bath	bathe

36

barely dare prepare rare share spare area

bare dare prepare rare share spare area

entirely surely rely

barrel

barred

wheelbarrow

borrow sorrow wheelbarrow growth

bath	father rather path gather bathe
bathe	bath
bathe	bath path father rather gather
battle	cattle
beach	each reach teach teacher
bead	lead leader ahead dead head instead
bean	
bear	tear wear clear dear ear hear near year early earn earth heard learn heart
beast	east Easter feast least
beat	beaten
beat	beaten eat meat neat seat theatre great
beaten	beat
beaten	beat eat meat neat seat theatre great
beautiful	beauty
beautiful	awful careful cheerful thankful wonderful
beauty	beautiful
became	came camel
because	cause
become	come welcome
bed	bedroom

meanwhile meant

bedroom	bed
bed**room**	broom room
bee	beef been
beef	bee been
been	bee beef
b**een**	between green queen seen
bef**ore**	more shore sore store
beg**an**	begin beginning begun
begin	beginning
begin	began beginning begun
beginning	begin
beginning	began begin begun
begun	began begin beginning
be**have**	have haven't
behavi**our**	
beh**ind**	find hind kind mind wind
being	
be**lie**ve	lie
be**long**	along long
be**long**	along long strong among

40

favour harbour labour neighbourhood journal fourteen
fourth yours courage sour

be**low**	**blow flow low slow clown**
be**lt**	**felt melt**
ben ch	
be**nd**	**friend lend send spend**
ben eath	
be**neath**	
be**neath**	
bene ath	
be**nt**	**lent plenty sent spent twenty went**
be**rry**	**cherry merry**
be**side**	**inside outside side**
be**st**	**contest nest rest test west question**
be**t**	**between**
be**tter**	**letter**
be**tt** er	**letter lettuce pretty**
bet ween	**bet**
betw**een**	**been green queen seen**
Bible	
bi**cycle**	**cycle tricycle**
bi**rd**	**third**
bi**rth**	**birthday**

beneath

bench

underneath

breathe underneath wreath breath death feather

enemy energy whenever

birthday	birth
bis**c**uit	fruit suit tracksuit quite
b**ite**	invite kite quite white write
bl**ack**	back pack quack sack track
bl**ade**	made shade spade
bl**ank**et	ankle bank drank
bl**ew**	few flew new newspaper sew
bl**ind**	
bl**ist**er	
bl**ist**er	
bl**ock**	clock lock o'clock
bl**ood**	flood
bl**oo**d	bloom
bl**oom**	blood
bl**oom**	gloomy
bl**oss**om	
bl**oss**om	
b**low**	below flow low slow clown
bl**ue**	glue true
b**oar**	

44

kindness remind indeed index industry

artist distant district minister mistake mistress scientist wrist listening

minister

loss

boss loss moss

cardboard

board	aboard cupboard
boast	
boast	
boat	coat goat oats throat
bodies	ladies dies
body	anybody everybody nobody somebody
boil	oil soil spoil
bolt	
bomb	comb
bone	alone telephone throne done none honey money one gone
book	cook hook look shook took snooker
booklet	
boot	root shoot foot
border	
born	corn corner horn morning worn
borrow	
borrow	
boss	
both	bother
bother	both

toast

toast oasis

colt

violet complete

afford cord ford record recorder

sorrow

barrow sorrow wheelbarrow growth

blossom loss moss

bother	another brother mother other
bothers	
bothers	
bottle	throttle
bottle	bottom throttle
bottom	bottle throttle
bough	
bought	brought fought nought ought thought drought
boulder	mould shoulder smoulder could should would
bound	around found ground mound playground pound round sound wound
boundary	
boundary	
bow	bowl
bowl	bow
box	
boy	cowboy enjoy joy toy
brain	
brain	
brake	rake

moth

breathe feather further therefore

thoughtful throughout

surround

February January military stationary

sprain

acquainted explain gain remain sprain

brake	bake baker cake lake make rake shake snake take wake
branch	
brass	
brave	cave gave save have
bread	already ready spread thread read
break	breakfast
break	steak speak
breakfast	break
breakfast	castle fast last master past
breast	
breath	
breath	
breath	
breath	
breathe	
breathe	
breathe	
breathe	
breathe	

brick	kick pick quick stick thick trick

pass association ass passenger

breath breathe

breathe

death feather beneath breathe underneath wreath

breathe wreath

breast breathe

breath

beneath underneath wreath breath death feather

wreath breath

breast breath

bothers feather further therefore

bridge	porridge ridge
bright	fright right (all right)
bright	delight fight flight fright light might night right sight tight tonight
bring	bringing during ring spring string
bring ing	bring during ring spring string
Brit ain	British
Britain	captain certain mountain
Brit ish	Britain
British	dish finish fish Irish wish
broad	
broad cast	
broke	awoke smoke spoke woke
broke n	
broom	bedroom room
brother	another mother other bother
brought	bought fought nought ought thought drought
brown	crown drown grown thrown
brow n	crown drown growl grow grown row throw thrown
brush	rush thrush

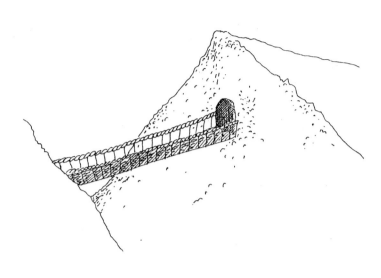

broadcast

broad

joke

brush	rush thrush bush push
bubble	
bucket	duck luck struck truck
build	built
built	build
bull	bulldozer full pull
bulldozer	bull full pull
bullet	
bump	jump pump
bunch	lunch
bundle	
bunny	funny sunny
buried	bury burn burnt burst
burn	burnt burst buried bury
burn	burnt return turn
burnt	burn burst buried bury
burst	burn burnt buried bury
burst	nurse purse
bury	buried burn burnt burst
bus	business busy
bush	push brush rush thrush

dull gull

idle

business	busy bus
busy	business bus
bu**t**	butter shut put
bu**tch**er	
bu**t**ter	but shut put
butter**fly**	
button	
b**uy**	guy

fetch hatch hitch patch pitch scratch
stitch

fly

mutton

cabb**age**	bandage cottage language manage message village age cage page rage stage
cabb**ag**e	bag
cabin	
cabinet	
ca**bine**t	
cafe	
c**age**	age cage page rage stage bandage cottage language manage message village
c**ake**	bake baker brake lake make rake shake snake take wake
cal**end**ar	
cal**end**ar	
c**alf**	half
c**all**	all hall small gallon shall valley allow (all right)
c**alm**	
c**alves**	halves
came	became camel
came**l**	became came
c**amera**	
c**amp**	damp lamp stamp

cabinet

cabin

continent engineer happiness mineral
vinegar miner nineteen outline pine vine
machinery magazine medicine

splendid

attend friendship independence independent pretend
splendid tender

palm salmon

ashamed flame frame lame tame

can	candle cannot canary canoe cane can't
canary	canoe can candle cannot cane can't
can **ary**	dictionary necessary secretary library
candle	can cannot canary canoe cane can't
c **andle**	bandage grand hand handkerchief handle sandals standard
c **andle**	handle
cane	can candle cannot canary canoe can't
cannot	can candle canary canoe cane can't
canoe	canary can candle cannot cane can't
can **oe**	shoe
can't	can candle cannot canary canoe cane
c **ape**	
capital	captain capture
captain	capital capture
cap **tain**	Britain certain mountain
capture	capital captain
cap **ture**	picture puncture
car	card
cara **van**	
caravan	

---

ape gape shape tape

---

advantage van

cardboard carpenter cart carve scar scarf
caring scarce scaring

---

card	car
c**ard**	hard hardly yard standard ward
card**boar**d	
cardboard	
c**ard**board	
care	careful careless scare
careful	care careless scare
care**ful**	awful beautiful cheerful thankful wonderful
careless	care careful scare
caring	
carpenter	
carp**enter**	
carri**age**	
c**arried**	married
c**arrier**	barrier
c**arry**	marry
cart	
c**art**	

62

boar

carpenter cart carve scar scarf caring
scarce scaring caravan

guard harden pardon regard afterwards backwards
forwards towards orchard

scarce scaring cardboard carpenter cart carve
scar scarf caravan

cardboard cart carve scar scarf caring
scarce scaring caravan

entertain entertainment

advantage average courage damage postage sausage
voyage

cardboard carpenter carve scar scarf caring
scarce scaring caravan

artist chart particular partner tart

carve

carve

case | base chase

cast

castle | fast last master past breakfast

cat | catch

catch | cat

catch | match watch

cattle | battle

caught | daughter naughty taught laughter

cause | because

cave | brave gave save have

ceiling

celeb**rate** | rate separate

cele**ry**

cele**ry**

cell

cell

cement | government moment

cent

cardboard carpenter cart scar scarf caring scarce scaring caravan

starve harvest wharves

fasten haste paste taste waste plastic

deceive

bakery discovery embroidery jewellery machinery mystery slippery stationery

election eleventh telegram telegraph

excellent

intelligent umbrella excellent jewellery traveller

centimetre

centi**metre**

centimetre

centime**tre**

cent**ime**tre

centi**met**re

central | centre century

cen**tre** | theatre

centre | central century

century | central centre

cer**tain** | Britain captain mountain

ch**ain** | again main pain paint plain

c**hair** | hair

ch**air** | air aircraft airport dairy fair fairly fairy hair pair

ch**alk** | stalk talk walk

ch**ance** | dance balance distance entrance

ch**ange** | danger strange orange

chap | chapter

chapter | chap

c**har**acter

metre

cent

litre metre

crime sometimes

metre metal metallic geometry method sometimes

harbour harden harness harvest chart orchard
share wharf wharves

char**acter**

charge | large

chart

chart

chase | base case

chat | hat that what hate

chatter | matter

cheap

cheap

cheer | deer queer

cheer**ful** | awful beautiful careful thankful wonderful

cheese | geese

cherry | berry merry

chest | orchestra

chew

chicken | thicken

chief | handkerchief mischief

chief | handkerchief mischief thief

child | children

child | wild children

attractive exactly manufacture subtract tract subtraction traction

artist cart particular partner tart

harbour harden harness harvest orchard share wharf wharves character

heap

heap weapon

crew jewel jewellery

children	child
children	child wild
chimney	
chin	
chocol**ate**	
ch**oice**	voice
choir	
ch**oose**	goose loose
cho**rus**	
c**hose**	hose those chosen whose
ch**ose**	close hose nose rose suppose those chosen lose whose
c**hosen**	chose hose those whose
chosen	chose close hose nose rose suppose those lose whose
Christ	Christmas
Christmas	Christ
church	churn
churn	church
circle	circular circus
circular	circle circus

70

machinery

immediately pirate private appreciate decorate skate state
statement whatever

crust trust

71

circus	circle circular
citizen	city
city	electricity
city	citizen
civil	
civilian	
cl aim	aim
c lass	glass lass
cl ass	glass grass assembly lass
c lay	lay play
cl ean	mean ocean
cl ear	dear ear hear near year bear tear wear early earn earth heard learn heart
cl iff	
cli mate	material mate
climate	climb
climb	climate
cl oak	oak soak
c lock	block lock o'clock
c lose	lose

civilian

civil

difficult stiff

73

close	chose hose nose rose suppose those chosen lose whose
cloth	clothes
clothes	cloth
cloud	aloud loud
cloud	aloud loud proud
clover	
clover	
clown	down town known own
clown	below blow flow low slow
coach	
coal	goal
coast	roast
coat	boat goat oats throat
cocoa	
coconut	
coffee	toffee
cold	fold gold hold old sold told
collar	
collect	
collect	

discovery overalls

overalls cove rove November discovery oven
shovel improve improvement

coconut

cocoa

college collect collection

collection collar college

object perfect project respect

coll ection

colle**ction**

coll ege

colo**ny**

colon y

col**our**

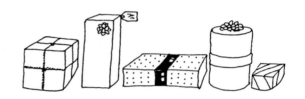

favourite honour neighbour journey flour hour our course court four pour your

co**l**t

co**mb**

bomb

come

become welcome

come

some home

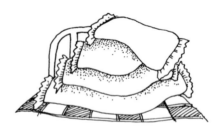

comfort

comfort able

comfor**table**

comm and

com**man**d

comm**and**

commerc e

comm erce

commerc ial

comm ercial

collect collar college

direction election protection section

collar collect collection

pony stony

lonely nylon

bolt

comfortable

comfort

stable unable

commercial committee community commerce

fisherman gentleman human manner manufacture

handful sandwich wander

commercial

command commercial committee community

commerce

command committee community commerce

commer**cial**

committee

common

comm**unity**

community

commun**ity**

company

compl**ete**

comp**lete**

conc**ert**

concr**ete**

cond**ition**

condition

c**ond**ition

condi**tion**

con**side**r

con**side**r

con**tain**

con**test**

cont**est**

---

company

---

common

---

test

best nest rest test west question

---

social

command commercial community commerce

opportunity unit unite

command commercial committee commerce

majority opportunity publicity quality quantity

concrete nineteen pretend

booklet violet

desert entertain entertainment fertile liberty property

complete nineteen pretend

exhibition

second

Monday diamond second

exhibition invention motion production

aside

aside guide provide stride tide embroidery

entertain entertainment obtain curtain fountain mountainous

continent

cont**ine**nt

conti**nue**

contin**ue**

continue

con**trol**

cook

cool

cop**per**

copy

cord

cord

core

core

corn

corner

corr**ect**

cost

petrol	
book hook look shook took snooker	
pool school stool tools wool	

born corner horn morning worn	
born corn horn morning worn	
elect electric electricity expect insect protect select subject	
frost lost almost ghost most post	

continue

cabinet engineer happiness mineral
vinegar miner nineteen outline pine vine
machinery magazine medicine

avenue

avenue due rescue statue Tuesday value

continent

opera operation perfect permission proper property
slippery temperature whisper

record recorder

afford border ford record recorder

score

ashore explore fore are score
therefore tore wore forever foreign

cost**ume**	
cottage	cotton
cott**age**	bandage cabbage language manage message village age cage page rage stage
cotton	cottage
c**ough**	although though enough rough tough plough
cou**gh**	could count county country couple cousin course court
c**ould**	should would boulder mould shoulder smoulder
cou**ld**	cough count county country couple cousin course court
cou**ncil**	
count	county country
c**ount**	amount county mount mountain
cou**nt**	county could cough country couple cousin course court
country	count county
cou**ntry**	couple cousin could cough count county course court
cou**nty**	count country could cough couple cousin course court
county	count country
cou**ple**	country cousin could cough count county course court

courage

cou**rage**

cour**age**

c**our**age

cou**r**age

c**our**se | court four pour your flour hour our colour favourite honour neighbour journey

course | court country couple cousin could cough count county

court | courteous

c**our**t | course four pour your flour hour our colour favourite honour neighbour journey

court | course country couple cousin could cough count county

courteous | court

cousin | country couple could cough count county course court

c**ove**

cover | discover

cover | discover government over

cow | cowboy

cowboy | cow

cowbo**y** | boy enjoy joy toy

average

advantage average carriage damage postage sausage voyage

behaviour favour harbour labour neighbourhood fourteen fourth yours journal sour

council

clover November overalls rove discovery oven shovel improve improvement

crack

crash

crawl

crayon

cream | dream ice-cream stream

creek | seek week

crept

crew

cricket | ticket wicket

cried | dried tried

cries | dries tries

crime

crime

criminal

cross | across crossing

crossing | across cross

crow | crowd crown

crowd | crown crow

crown | crowd crow

crown | brown drown grown thrown

attack backwards jacket lack stack tack

ash flash lash splash ashamed ashore

hawk lawyer awake

pray prayer ray

September swept

chew jewel jewellery

criminal

sometimes centimetre

crime

87

crown	brown drown growl grow grown row throw thrown
cruel	fuel
crumb	
crust	
crust	
cry	dry try
cube	
cube	
cubic	
cup	cupboard
cupboard	cup
cupboard	aboard board
cure	
cure	
curly	
current	
curtain	
curtain	
cushion	
cycle	bicycle tricycle

umbrella

trust

trust chorus

cubic

tube

cube

pure figure surely

curly curtain

curtain cure

rent

fountain mountainous contain entertain entertainment obtain

curly cure

dad	daddy
daddy	dad
daily	
dairy	air aircraft airport chair fair fairly fairy hair pair
daisy	praise raise waist
damage	
d**ama**ge	
damp	camp lamp stamp
dance	chance balance distance entrance
danger	change strange orange
d**anger**ous	
danger**ous**	
dan**ger**ous	
d**are**	
d**ar**k	bark mark market park
dark**ness**	
d**ate**	ate gate hate late mate plate
d**augh**ter	laughter
d**augh**ter	caught naughty taught laughter
d**awn**	lawn yawn

hail railway

advantage average carriage courage postage sausage voyage

pyjamas

stranger anger

jealous mountainous murderous nervous

murderous hero zero

bare barely prepare rare share spare area

goodness happiness harness kindness sickness

day	holiday today
dead	ahead head instead bead lead leader
deaf	leaf
deal	heal meal real seal health
dear	clear ear hear near year bear tear wear early earn earth heard learn heart
death	
deceive	
December	
December	
decide	divide hide ride side slide wide
deck	
decorate	

deed	
deed	
deep	keep sheep steep
deer	cheer queer
degree	
delicious	
delicious	

breath feather beneath breathe underneath wreath

ceiling

September November

September October November

neck speck wreck

appreciate skate state statement chocolate immediately private pirate whatever

indeed

indeed succeed

agree agreement greeting

anxious serious various

delighted deliver model

delight	flight light
delight	bright fight flight fright light might night right sight tight tonight
delighted	
delighted	
deliver	
deliver	
dense	
dental	accident dentist
dentist	accident dental
deposit	positive position
desert	
design	sign signal
destination	
destination	
destroy	
destroy	
develop	
develop	

knight lightning midnight mighty

delicious deliver model

attractive expensive forgive motive native alive

delicious delighted model

sense

concert entertain entertainment fertile liberty
property

appreciation association formation information irrigation
multiplication occupation operation plantation recreation
stationary stationery

destroy harvest honest

destination harvest honest

oysters voyage

development

event level prevent eleventh seventeen seventh
forever whatever whenever eve fever

development

develop**ment**

diam**ond**

dia**mon**d

diction**ary** | necessary secretary canary library

di**e** | lie pie tie field

dies | bodies ladies

difference | different

differ**ence** | experience science fence pence

different | difference

difficult

diffi**cult**

digest

di**ning**

d**inner** | winner

dir**ection**

di**re**ction

d**ir**t | dirty shirt thirty

d**irt**y | dirt shirt thirty

develop

agreement amusement appointment argument disappointment entertainment equipment improvement instrument ointment payment refreshment settlement statement

second condition Monday

lemon lemonade salmon Monday

cliff stiff

agriculture multiplication result

lightning listening shining

collection election protection section

entire entirely tire umpire

dis**appear**

disap**pear**

dis**appear**ance

disap**pear**ance

disappear**ance**

dis**appoint**

disapp**oint**

dis**appoint**ment

disapp**oint**ment

disappoint**ment**

disc

disco

disco

dis**cover**

disc**over**

discovery

discovery

disc**over**y

disc**ove**ry

cover

cover government over

appear appearance disappearance

appear appearance disappearance spear pear

appear appearance disappear

appear appearance disappear spear pear

appearance importance instance nuisance

appoint appointment disappointment

appoint appointment disappointment ointment

appoint appointment disappoint

appoint appointment disappoint ointment

agreement amusement appointment argument
development entertainment equipment improvement
instrument ointment payment refreshment settlement
statement

disco discovery

discovery

disc discovery

disco

disc disco

clover overalls

oven shovel clover overalls cove rove November
improve improvement

discov**ery**

dis**ease**	please
d**ish**	British finish fish Irish wish
dis**obey**	obey
disob**ey**	grey obey they eye
dist**ance**	balance entrance chance dance
d**ist**ant	

dis**tant**

dist**ant**

di**strict**

d**ist**rict

d**itch**	witch
d**ive**	arrive drive driver five knives wives give live river
div**ide**	decide hide ride side slide wide
di**vision**	television
doc**tor**	editor tractor visitor
d**oes**	doesn't goes potatoes toes shoes
d**oes**n't	does goes potatoes toes shoes

bakery celery embroidery jewellery machinery
mystery slippery stationery

artist blister district minister mistake
mistress scientist wrist listening

accountant

accountant vacant lantern advantage plantation quantity
meant

strict

artist blister distant minister mistake
mistress scientist wrist listening

d**og**	frog
d**oing**	going
done	undone
d**one**	none honey money one alone bone telephone throne gone
don**key**	key monkey
d**on't**	won't
d**oor**	floor outdoors poor
d**ouble**	trouble
down	downstairs
d**own**	clown town known own
downstairs	down
down**stairs**	stairs upstairs
d**ozen**	frozen
dr**ago**n	ago
dr**ank**	ankle bank blanket
draw	drawer
d**raw**	drawer raw straw
dr**aw**	drawer law paw saw see-saw straw
drawer	draw
d**raw**er	draw raw straw

103

drawer	draw law paw saw see-saw straw
dread	
dread	
dream	cream ice-cream stream
dress	address
drew	grew threw
dried	cried tried
dries	cries tries
drift	gift lift
drink	pink think
drive	arrive dive driver five knives wives give live river
driver	river
driver	arrive dive drive five knives wives give live river
drop	
drought	bought brought fought nought ought thought
drove	stove move prove above glove love lovely
drown	brown crown grown thrown
drown	brown crown growl grow grown row throw thrown

reader

steady reader

proper property

drunk	trunk
dry	cry try
duck	bucket luck struck truck
due	
dull	
dumb	thumb number
during	bring bringing ring spring string
dust	just justice must
duty	
dwell	swell well
dye	
dye ing	
dying	lying

avenue continue rescue statue Tuesday value

gull bullet

dyeing

dye

A B C D E F G H I J K L M N O P Q R S T U V W X Y Z

each	beach reach teach teacher
eagle	
ear	clear dear hear near year bear tear wear early earn earth heard learn heart
early	earn earth heard learn clear dear ear hear near year bear tear wear heart
earn	learn
earn	early earth heard learn clear dear ear hear near year bear tear wear heart
earth	early earn heard learn clear dear ear hear near year bear tear wear heart
easily	easy reason season
east	beast Easter feast least
Easter	beast east feast least
easy	easily reason season
eat	beat beaten meat neat seat theatre great
eave	
echo	
edge	hedge
edi**tor**	doctor tractor visitor

league

heave weave heaven

egg

eight | eighty weight height

eight | eighty neighbour weigh weight height

eighteen

eighteen

eigh **teen**

eighth

eighth

eighty | eight weight height

either | neither

elect | electric electricity select

el **ect** | correct electric electricity expect insect protect select subject

el **ection**

election

electric | elect electricity select

el **ect**ric | correct elect electricity expect insect protect select subject

electri **city** | city

electricity | elect electric select

el **ect**ricity | correct elect electric expect insect protect select subject

110

eighth freight

eighth freight neigh neighbourhood

thirteen fourteen fifteen sixteen seventeen nineteen

eighteen freight

eighteen freight neigh neighbourhood

collection direction protection section

eleventh telegram telegraph celery

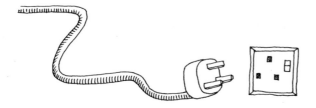

eleph**ant**	giant infants ant pant plant want
el**even**	seven seventy even evening
el**even**th	
ele**ven**th	
el**eve**nth	
eleventh	
el**s**e	also
embro**ide**ry	
embroid**ery**	
empty	
enemy	
e**ner**gy	

energy	
en**gine**	imagine
eng**ine**	imagine fine line mine nine shine sunshine wine machine
engine	England English
eng**ine**er	

seventeen seventh event prevent

seventh event invent inventor prevent vent
seventeen adventure invention

seventeen seventh event prevent forever whatever
whenever develop level eve fever

election telegram telegraph celery

aside guide provide stride tide consider

bakery celery discovery jewellery machinery
mystery slippery stationery

beneath energy whenever

machinery miner mineral nervous owner partner
prisoner stationery

beneath enemy whenever

cabinet continent happiness mineral
vinegar miner nineteen outline pine vine
machinery magazine medicine

engin**eer**

Eng**land** | Ireland island Scotland land

Eng land | English engine

Eng lish | England engine

en**joy** | boy cowboy joy toy

en**ough** | rough tough cough although though plough

entertain

enter**tain**

ent**ert** ain

enter tain

entertain ment

entertain**ment**

enter**tain** ment

enter tainment

ent**ert** ainment

entire

en**tire**

en**tir** e

114

pioneer steer

entertainment

contain entertainment obtain curtain fountain
mountainous

concert desert entertainment fertile liberty property

entertainment carpenter

entertain

agreement amusement appointment argument
development disappointment equipment improvement
instrument ointment payment refreshment settlement
statement

contain entertain obtain curtain fountain
mountainous

entertain carpenter

concert desert entertain fertile liberty property

entirely

entirely tire

entirely tire stir

ent**ire**

entirely

enti**rely**

en**tirely**

en**tire**ly

ent**ire**ly

entr**ance**

envel**ope**

e**qual**

eq**ual**

equip

e**quip**

equipment

equip**ment**

balance distance chance dance

e**qui**pment

error

e**rror**

esc**ape**

e**special**ly

grapes

special

entirely tire umpire direction

entire

barely surely rely

entire tire

entire tire stir

entire tire umpire direction

opera operation proper property

acquainted quality quantity quarrel

gradual gradually habitual quality

equipment

equipment liquid

equip

agreement amusement appointment argument development disappointment entertainment improvement instrument ointment payment refreshment settlement statement

equip liquid

terror

horror mirror terror

Europe	rope
Europe	hope rope
eve	
even	evening eleven seven seventy
even ing	even eleven seven seventy
event	
event	
eve nt	
ever	however never every several
every	very
ever y	several ever however never
everybody	anybody body nobody somebody
everyone	anyone one someone
everything	anything nothing something thing
everywhere	anywhere nowhere somewhere where
exactly	
exam	
examination	nation national

fever event prevent eleventh seventeen seventh forever whatever whenever develop level

prevent eleventh seventeen seventh

invent inventor prevent vent seventeen eleventh seventh adventure invention

prevent eleventh seventeen seventh forever whatever whenever develop level eve fever

attractive character manufacture subtract tract subtraction traction

example

examin**ation**	invitation nation population station national
example	
ex**cell**ent	
ex**cell**ent	
excel**lent**	
except	exciting excuse
exch**ange**	
exciting	except excuse
exc**use**	use useful museum
excuse	except exciting
exerc**ise**	
exhibit	
exhi**bit**	
exhib**ition**	
exhibition	
exhibi**tion**	
exhi**bit**ion	
exit	
exp**ect**	correct elect electric electricity insect protect select subject
expens**ive**	

exam

cell

cell intelligent umbrella jewellery traveller

silent

angel anger

organise realise

exhibition

habit habitual exhibition

condition

exhibit

condition invention motion production

exhibit habit habitual

attractive forgive motive native deliver alive

exper **ience**

experi **ence**

expl **ain**

expl **ore**

ex **press**ed

exp **ress**ed

extra

extremely

extr **emely**

eye

science

difference science fence pence

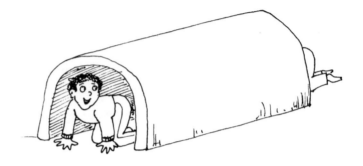

disobey they grey

acquainted brain gain remain sprain

ashore core fore ore score
therefore tore wore foreign forever

press

press progress mistress

extremely

extra

agreement amusement improvement settlement statement

face	surface
face	fireplace lace place race space palace surface
fact	factory satisfactory
factory	satisfactory
factory	fact satisfactory
fail	jail mail nail rail sail snail tail trail
fair	fairly fairy
fair	air aircraft airport chair dairy fairly fairy hair pair
fairly	fair fairy
fairly	air aircraft airport chair dairy fair fairy hair pair
fairy	air aircraft airport chair dairy fair fairly hair pair
familiar	family famous
family	familiar famous
famous	familiar family
fancy	
far	farm farmer farther
far	farther jar war
farm	farmer

ancient

far m	far farmer farther
farm	alarm arm army farmer harm warm
farm er	farm
far mer	far farm farther
farm er	alarm arm army farm harm warm
far ther	far farm farmer
far ther	far jar war
fast	last master past breakfast castle
faste n	
fast en	
father	grandfather
fath er	rather bath path gather bathe
favour	
favour ite	colour honour neighbour journey flour hour our course court four pour your
fear	
feast	beast east Easter least
feath er	
feathe r	
February	
feed	need needle seed

haste paste taste waste

caste haste paste taste waste plastic

behaviour harbour labour neighbourhood journal fourteen fourth yours courage sour

nearly learned search wearing

breath death breathe beneath underneath wreath

bothers further breathe therefore

boundary January military stationary

feel	steel wheel
feet	meet sheet street sweet teeth
fellow	yellow
felt	belt melt
fence	pence difference experience science
fertile	
fertile	
fertile	
fetch	
fever	
fever	
few	new newspaper blew flew sew
field	die lie pie tie
fierce	
fifteen	
fifteen	
fifth	
fight	bright delight flight fright light might night right sight tight tonight
figure	

tile

concert desert entertain entertainment liberty property

meanwhile missile smile tile silence silent

butcher hatch hitch patch pitch scratch
stitch

forever whatever whenever

eve event prevent eleventh seventeen seventh
forever whatever whenever develop level

pierce

thirteen fourteen sixteen seventeen eighteen nineteen

rift swift thrifty fifth

fifteen rift swift thrifty

cure pure surely

fill	ill still will
film	
final	finally
final	find finish
finally	final
find	final finish
find	behind hind kind mind wind
fine	line mine nine shine sunshine wine engine imagine machine
finger	singer ginger
finish	final find
finish	British dish fish Irish wish
fire	wire
firep**lace**	lace place palace
firepl**ace**	face lace place race space palace surface
first	thirsty
fish	British dish finish Irish wish
fisher**man**	
f**ish**erman	
five	arrive dive drive driver knives wives give live river

gentleman human command manner manufacture

foolish furnish goldfish varnish

fix	mix six sixty
flag	flat
flame	
flame	
flash	
flash	
flat	flag
flew	blew few new newspaper sew
flies	lies
flight	delight light
flight	bright delight fight fright light might night right sight tight tonight
float	
float	
flock	
flood	blood
floor	door outdoors poor
flour	hour our course court four pour your colour favourite honour neighbour journey
flow	below blow low slow clown
flower	lower slower
fly	

lame

ashamed frame lame tame camera

lash splash

ash crash lash splash ashamed ashore

loaf loaves

flock

float

butterfly

f oam	roam
f old	cold gold hold old sold told
f olk	
f ollow	hollow
f ond	pond London
f ood	good goodbye stood wood
fool	
f ool	
foolish	
f oolish	
fool ish	

f oot	boot root shoot
footnball	footpath
foot ball	ball snowball balloon
foot path	path
footpath	football
for	forget forgot forgotten forest
forced	
ford	
f ord	

yolk

foolish

foolish woollen

fool

fool woollen

fisherman furnish goldfish varnish

ford fore forever forgive format formation
forwards foreign

afford

afford border cord record recorder

ford

fore

f**ore**

fore

fo**reign**

f**ore**ign

foreign

foreign

---

fo**rest**   arrest interested rest

---

forest   for forget forgot forgotten

---

for**ever**

for**eve**r

f**ore**ver

forever

forever

---

forget   forgot forgotten for forest

---

forg**ive**

forced fore forever forgive format formation
forwards foreign

therefore forever foreign

ashore core explore ore score
therefore tore wore foreign forever

forced ford forever forgive format formation
forwards foreign

reign

ashore core explore fore ore score
therefore tore wore forever

fore therefore forever

forced ford fore forever forgive format
formation forwards

whatever whenever fever

whatever whenever eleventh seventeen seventh event
prevent develop level eve fever

ashore core explore fore ore score
therefore tore wore foreign

fore therefore foreign

forced ford fore forgive format formation
forwards foreign

attractive expensive motive native deliver alive

for give

forgot	forgotten
for got	forget forgotten for forest
forgot ten	forgot
for gotten	forget forgot for forest
fork	work
form	storm worm

form at

for mat

formation

form ation

for mation

fort	fortune forty
fort une	fort forty
fort y	fort fortune

for**wards**

for wards

forced ford fore forever format formation
forwards foreign

formation inform information

forced ford fore forever forgive formation
forwards foreign

appreciation association destination information irrigation
multiplication occupation operation plantation recreation
stationary stationery

format inform information

forced ford fore forever forgive format
forwards foreign

afterwards backwards towards

forced ford fore forever forgive format
formation foreign

forwards

fought	bought brought nought ought thought drought
found	around bound ground mound playground pound round sound wound

fountain

fountain

four	course court pour your flour hour our colour favourite honour neighbour journey

fourteen

fourteen

fourth

frame

free	freedom freeze
freedom	kingdom
freedom	free freeze
freeze	free freedom

freight

freight

fresh

afterwards backwards orchard towards cardboard guard
harden pardon regard

curtain mountainous contain entertain entertainment
obtain

account accountant mountainous

thirteen fifteen sixteen seventeen eighteen nineteen

fourth yours behaviour favour harbour
labour neighbourhood journal courage sour

fourteen yours behaviour favour harbour
labour neighbourhood journal courage sour

ashamed flame lame tame camera

eighteen eighth

eighteen eighth neigh neighbourhood

refresh refreshment

Fri**day**	
fried	
fri**end**	bend lend send spend
fri**end**ship	
fries	
fr**ight**	bright delight fight flight light might night right sight tight tonight
fright	bright right (all right)
fr**og**	dog
frog	from frost front
from	frog frost front
front	frog from frost
fr**ont**	month
frost	frog from front
frost	cost lost almost most ghost post
froze	frozen
frozen	froze
fr**ozen**	dozen
fr**uit**	suit tracksuit biscuit quite
fuel	cruel
f**ull**	bull bulldozer pull

Saturday Sunday Monday Tuesday Wednesday Thursday

hurried

attend calendar independence independent pretend splendid tender

hurries lorries

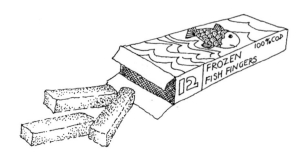

fume	perfume
funnel	tunnel
funny	bunny sunny
fur	
furnish	
furn**ish**	
furni**ture**	

furniture	
furry	hurry
further	
fur**ther**	
fuse	
fuse	
fu**ture**	

furnish furniture further

fur furniture further

fisherman foolish goldfish varnish

adventure agriculture future manufacture moisture nature temperature

fur furnish further

fur furnish furniture

bothers feather breathe therefore

refuse

amuse amusement muse refuse

adventure agriculture furniture manufacture moisture nature temperature

A
B
C
D
E
F
G
H
I
J
K
L
M
N
O
P
Q
R
S
T
U
V
W
X
Y
Z

g**ain**	
g**all** on	shall valley all call hall small allow (all right)
g**ame**	name same
g**ape**	
ga**rage**	rage
g**ar** age	garden sugar
g**ar** den	garage sugar
g**as**	has hasn't was wasn't
g**ate**	ate date hate late mate plate
g**ath** er	bath father path rather bathe
g**ave**	brave cave save have
g**eese**	cheese
g**en** eral	gentle
gent	
g**en** tle	general
gentle**man**	
gent leman	
gent ly	
geo**graph** y	paragraph
geo**met** ry	
geo metry	

acquainted brain explain remain sprain

ape cape shape tape

gentleman gently intelligent

fisherman human command manner manufacture

gent gently intelligent

gent gentleman intelligent

centimetre metre metal metallic method sometimes

pigeon

geome try	
germ	term
ghost	almost most post cost frost lost
giant	elephant infants ant pant plant want
gift	drift lift
ginger	finger singer
girl	whirl
give	live river arrive dive drive driver five knives wives
glad	lad ladies lady
glass	class lass
glass	class grass assembly lass
gloom y	bloom
glove	love lovely
glove	above love lovely drove stove move prove
glue	blue true
goal	coal
goat	boat coat oats throat
goes	potatoes toes does doesn't shoes
going	doing
gold	cold fold hold old sold told

sometimes women

golden

g**old**en

gol**den**

goldfish

g**old**fish

goldf**ish**

g**olf**

g**one**

done none honey money one alone
bone telephone throne

g**ood**

goodbye stood wood food

g**ood**bye

good stood wood food

good**ness**

g**ood**ness

g**oose**

loose choose

g**overn**ment

cover discover over

govern**ment**

moment cement

g**rabb**ed

rabbit

grace**ful**

grade

gr**ad**e

gradual

goldfish

goldfish household

harden wooden

golden

golden household

fisherman foolish furnish varnish

wolf

darkness happiness harness kindness sickness

hood neighbourhood wooden

handful playful successful thoughtful

gradual gradually

lemonade trade reader

gradually grade

grad**ual**

gradually

grad**ual**ly

gr**ai**n	rain rainbow train
grand	grandfather grandmother
gr**and**	bandage candle grandfather grandmother hand handkerchief handle sandals standard
grand**father**	father
grand father	grand grandmother
grand**mother**	mother
grand mother	grand grandfather
gr**ape** s	escape
graph	
gr**ap** h	
gr**ass**	class glass assembly lass
gr**ave**	
gr**avel**	travel
gr**az** e	
gr**ease**	
gr**eas** e	
gr**eat**	beat beaten eat meat neat seat theatre

gradually habitual equal quality

gradual grade

gradual habitual equal quality

photograph telegraph

photograph telegraph rapid rapidly wrap

slave avenue average traveller

lazy

increase pleased tease

increase measles peas pleased tease teaspoon

greedy	green
green	greedy
gr**een**	been between queen seen
greeting	
g**rew**	drew threw
gr**ey**	disobey obey they eye
g**round**	around playground round
g**round**	around bound found mound playground pound round sound wound
gr**oup**	soup
grow	grown growl
g**row**	grown row throw thrown brown crown drown growl
growl	grow grown
g**row**l	brown crown drown grow grown row throw thrown
grown	grow growl
g**rown**	thrown brown crown drown
g**row**n	grow row throw thrown brown crown drown growl
growth	
gu**ard**	

agree agreement degree

barrow borrow sorrow wheelbarrow

cardboard harden pardon regard afterwards backwards
forwards towards orchard

guess	guessed guest
guessed	guess guest
guest	guess guessed
gu**ide**	
g**ull**	
g**uy**	buy

aside provide stride tide consider embroidery

dull bullet

habit	
ha**bit**	
habitual	
ha**bit**ual	
habit**ual**	
had	hadn't
hadn't	had
h**ail**	
hair	chair
h**air**	air aircraft airport chair dairy fair fairly fairy pair
h**alf**	calf
hall	shall
h**all**	all call small gallon shall valley allow (all right)
h**alves**	calves
hammer	
hand	handkerchief
h**and**	bandage candle grand handkerchief handle sandals standard
h**and**ful	
hand**ful**	
handkerchief	hand

habitual

exhibit habitual exhibition

habit

exhibit habit exhibition

gradual gradually equal quality

daily railway

sandwich command wander

graceful playful successful thoughtful

handker**chief**	chief mischief
h**and** kerchief	bandage candle grand hand handle sandals standard
handker**chief**	chief mischief thief
h**andle**	candle
h**and** le	bandage candle grand hand handkerchief sandals standard
h**ang**	bang rang sang
happen	happy
h**app**en	apple
happily	
happiness	
happi**ness**	
happi**ne**ss	

hap**pine**ss	
hap**pin**ess	
happy	happen
har**bour**	
har bour	
har**bour**	

happiness unhappy

happily unhappy

darkness goodness harness kindness sickness

cabinet continent engineer mineral
vinegar miner nineteen outline pine vine
machinery magazine medicine

pine

spin pine

labour neighbourhood

harden harness harvest chart orchard share
wharf wharves character

behaviour favour labour neighbourhood journal fourteen
fourth yours courage sour

hard	card hardly yard standard ward
harden	
harden	
harden	
harden	
hardly	hard card yard standard ward
harm	alarm arm army farm farmer warm
harness	
harness	
harp	harpoon sharp
harpoon	harp sharp
harvest	
harvest	
harvest	
has	hasn't gas was wasn't
hasn't	has gas was wasn't
haste	
haste	
hat	chat that what hate

orchard

golden wooden

harbour harness harvest chart orchard share
wharf wharves character

cardboard guard pardon regard afterwards backwards
forwards towards orchard

darkness goodness happiness kindness sickness

harbour harden harvest chart orchard share
wharf wharves character

honest destination destroy

harden harbour harness chart orchard share
wharf wharves character

carve starve wharves

paste taste waste fasten

paste taste waste cast fasten plastic

h **atch**

ha **tch**

hate	chat that what hat
hate	ate gate date late mate plate
h**aul**	
h**aunt**	aunt auntie
h**aunt**	autumn aunt auntie
have	haven't behave
h**ave**	brave cave gave save
haven't	have behave
h**awk**	
head	ahead headteacher
h**ead**	ahead dead instead bead lead leader
headteacher	ahead head
heal	health healthy
h**eal**	deal meal real seal health
health	healthy heal
h**eal**th	deal heal meal real seal
healthy	health heal
heap	

patch scratch

butcher fetch hitch patch pitch scratch stitch

August author saucepan sausage

crawl lawyer awake

cheap

heap	
hear	heard heart
hear	clear dear ear near year bear tear wear early earn earth heard learn heart
heard	hear heart
heard	early earn earth learn clear dear ear hear near year bear tear wear heart
heart	hear heard
heart	clear dear ear hear near year bear tear wear early earn earth heard learn
heat	
heat	
heave	
heaven	
heavy	leave
hedge	edge
heel	
heel	
height	eight eighty weight
height	eighty neighbour weigh weight
held	help

cheap weapon

wheat

treat treaty wheat recreation

eave weave heaven

eave heave weave

wheelbarrow

kneel wheelbarrow

A B C D E F G H I J K L M N O P Q R S T U V W X Y Z

help	held
hen	then when
herd	
herd	
here	there where
h ere	there where were
hero	
h ero	
her self	himself itself myself self yourself
h ide	decide divide ride side slide wide
h igh	sigh
high way	
h ike	like
him self	herself itself myself self yourself
h ind	behind find kind mind wind
h ired	tired
his	history this whistle
h issed	missed
hi story	story
history	his this whistle
h itch	

168

shepherd

hero

herd

zero dangerous murderous

railway sway

pitch stitch

hi**tch**

hobby

h**oe**

h**old** .   cold fold gold old sold told

hole   whole

hole   pole tadpole whole

holi**day**   day today

h**ollow**   follow

h**ome**   come some

hon**est**

h**one**st

h**oney**   money

h**one**y   money done none one alone bone
telephone throne gone

hon**our**   colour favourite neighbour journey flour
hour our course court four pour your

hood

h**ood**

h**ook**   book cook look shook took snooker

h**ope**   rope Europe

hope   shop

butcher fetch hatch patch pitch scratch
stitch

tomatoes poet poetry

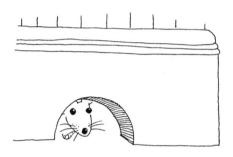

harvest destination destroy

prisoner stationery pioneer shone lonely stone
tone zone

neighbourhood

goodness neighbourhood wooden

horn	born corn corner morning worn
horror	
horror	
horse	worse
hose	chose those chosen whose
hose	chose close nose rose suppose those chosen lose whose
hospital	
hot	shot hotel
hotel	hot shot
hour	flour our course court four pour your colour favourite honour neighbour journey
house	mouse
household	
household	
how	anyhow however somehow show
however	anyhow how somehow show
however	ever never every several
human	
hundred	red
hundred	hung hungry hunt
hung	hundred hungry hunt

error mirror terror

lorries

pitch

golden goldfish

trousers

fisherman gentleman command manner manufacture

hung	sung hungry
hungry	hundred hung hunt
hungry	hung sung
hungry	angry
hunt	hundred hung hungry
hunt	until
hurl	hurt
hurried	
hurries	
hurry	furry
hurt	hurl
husband	band bandage

fried

lorries fries

175

ice

iceberg

ice-cream | cream dream stream

ice-cream | mice nice rice twice justice office officer practice police policeman

I'd | I'll I'm I've

idea | ideally

ideally | idea

idle

ill | fill still will

I'll | I'd I'm I've

I'm | I'd I'll I've

imagine | engine

imagine | engine fine line mine nine shine sunshine wine machine

immediately

immediately

immediately

import

import

importance

advice iceberg price spice notice service

advice ice price spice notice service

bundle

media

appreciate appreciation

chocolate pirate private appreciate decorate skate state statement whatever

importance

importance support transport opportunity

import

im **port** ance

import **ance**

im **port** ant   airport port report sport

im **possible**   possible

improve

impr **ove**

improve ment

improve **ment**

impr **ove** ment

improv **eme** nt

inch   pinch

include

incr **ease**

incr **eas** e

in **deed**

ind **eed**

ind eed

independ **ence**

import support transport opportunity

appearance disappearance instance nuisance

improvement

improvement discovery oven shovel clover overalls cove rove November

improve

agreement amusement appointment argument development disappointment entertainment equipment instrument ointment payment refreshment settlement statement

improve discovery oven shovel clover overalls cove rove November

agreement amusement settlement statement extremely

grease pleased tease

grease measles peas pleased tease teaspoon

deed

deed succeed

index industry blind kindness remind

absence silence

indep**end**ence

indep**end**ent

index

industry

inf**ants**

inf**ants**

inform

in**form**

information

inform**ation**

in**form**ation

ink

ins**ect**

in**side**

inst**ance**

inst**ead**

instru**ment**

ants

elephant giant ant pant plant want

correct elect electric electricity expect
protect select subject

beside outside side

ahead dead head bead lead leader

attend calendar friendship independent pretend
splendid tender

attend calendar friendship independence pretend
splendid tender

indeed industry blind kindness remind

indeed index blind kindness remind

information

format formation information

inform

appreciation association destination formation irrigation
multiplication occupation operation plantation recreation
stationary stationery

format formation inform

shrink sink

appearance disappearance importance nuisance

agreement amusement appointment argument
development disappointment entertainment equipment
improvement ointment payment refreshment settlement
statement

instr**u**ment

int**elli**gent

intelli**gent**

intell**ige**nt

inte**rest**ed

invent

in**vent**

invention

in**vent**ion

inven**tion**

inventor

in**vent**or

invit**ation**

inv**ite**

Ire**land**

Ir**ish**

iron

irrig**ation**

arrest rest forest

examination nation population station national

bite kite quite white write

England island Scotland land

British dish finish fish wish

argument costume

cell umbrella excellent jewellery traveller

gent gentle gentleman

pigeon

inventor invention

event inventor prevent vent seventeen eleventh
seventh adventure invention

invent inventor

adventure event invent inventor prevent vent
seventeen eleventh seventh

condition exhibition motion production

invent invention

event invent prevent vent seventeen eleventh
seventh adventure invention

appreciation association destination formation information
multiplication occupation operation plantation recreation
stationary stationery

island	isn't
is**land**	England Ireland Scotland land
isn't	island
it**self**	herself himself myself self yourself
I've	I'd I'll I'm

A
B
C
D
E
F
G
H
I
J
K
L
M
N
O
P
Q
R
S
T
U
V
W
X
Y
Z

jacket

jail | fail mail nail rail sail snail
tail trail

January

jar | far farther war

jealous

jealous

jelly | shell smell spell swell

jewel

jewel

jewellery

jewellery

jewellery

jewellery

join | point

joke

jolly | lolly

journal

journey | colour honour favourite neighbour flour
hour our course court four pour your

joy | boy cowboy enjoy toy

attack backwards crack lack stack tack

boundary February military stationary

dangerous mountainous murderous nervous

wealth wealthy realise really steal

jewellery

chew crew jewellery

jewel

bakery celery discovery embroidery machinery mystery slippery stationery

excellent traveller cell intelligent umbrella

chew crew jewel

broken

behaviour favour harbour labour neighbourhood fourteen fourth yours courage sour

judge	
juice	juicy
juicy	juice
July	
jump	bump pump
June	
jungle	junior
junior	jungle
junior	senior
just	justice
just	dust justice must
justice	just
justice	dust just must
justice	office officer practice ice-cream mice nice rice twice police policeman

badge knowledge ledge

June

July

k **een**	
k **eep**	deep sheep steep
kennel	
k **ept**	slept
k **ettle**	
key	donkey monkey
k **ick**	brick pick quick stick thick trick
k **ill**	
k **ind**	behind find hind mind wind
k **ind**ness	
kind **ness**	
king	asking baking kingdom making taking
kingdom	asking baking king making taking
king **dom**	freedom
k **iss**	
kitchen	kitten
k **ite**	bite invite quite white write
kitten	kitchen
knee	
knee	

screen

settlement settler

mill pillow

blind remind indeed index industry

darkness goodness happiness harness sickness

scissors

kneel

kneel knelt knight knit knob knot
knowledge

kneel

kneel

kneel

knelt

knelt

knew   new newspaper

knife   life wife

knight

knight

knit

knives   arrive dive drive driver five wives
     give live river

knob

knot

knot

know   known

know   known snow now

knowledge

knee

heel wheelbarrow

knee knelt knight knit knob knot
knowledge

knee kneel knight knit knob knot
knowledge

shelter

delighted lightning midnight mighty

knee kneel knelt knit knob knot
knowledge

knee kneel knelt knight knob knot
knowledge

knee kneel knelt knight knit knot
knowledge

knee kneel knelt knight knit knob
knowledge

notice

ledge

knowle**dge**

kn owledge

---

know n   know

---

know n   know snow now

---

kn**own**   own clown down town

badge judge ledge

knee kneel knelt knight knit knob
knot

labour

labour

lace	fireplace place palace
lace	face fireplace place race space palace surface
lack	
lad	glad ladies lady
ladder	add addition address
ladies	glad lad lady
ladies	bodies dies
lady	glad lad ladies
laid	afraid maid paid raid said
lake	bake baker brake cake make rake shake snake take wake
lame	
lame	
lamp	camp damp stamp
land	England Ireland island Scotland
language	bandage cabbage cottage manage message village age cage page rage stage
lantern	

harbour neighbourhood

behaviour favour harbour neighbourhood journal fourteen fourth yours courage sour

attack backwards crack jacket stack tack

flame

ashamed flame frame tame camera

plantation

lant ern

large	charge
lash	
lash	
lass	class glass
lass	assembly class glass grass
last	fast master past breakfast castle
late	later plate
late	ate date gate hate mate plate
late r	late plate
later	water
laugh	laughter
laugh ter	laugh
laughter	daughter
laught er	caught daughter naughty taught
law	draw drawer paw saw see-saw straw
lawn	dawn yawn
law yer	
lay	clay play
laz y	

accountant distant vacant advantage plantation quantity meant

flash splash

ash crash flash splash ashamed ashore

crawl hawk awake

graze

lead	leader
lead	bead leader ahead dead head instead
leader	lead
leader	bead lead ahead dead head instead
leaf	deaf
league	
league	
learn	earn
learn	earn early earth heard clear dear ear hear near year bear tear wear heart
learned	
least	beast east Easter feast
leather	weather
leave	heavy
ledge	
ledge	
left	theft
legal	
lemon	
lemon	
lemonade	

tongue argue

eagle

search fear nearly wearing

knowledge

badge judge knowledge

telegram telegraph

lemonade

diamond lemonade salmon Monday

lemon

le**mon**ade	
lemon**ade**	
l**end**	bend friend send spend
l**ength**	
l**ent**	plenty
l**ent**	bent plenty sent spent twenty went
less	lesson unless
lesson	less unless
l**etter**	better
l**etter**	better lettuce pretty
l**ett**uce	better letter pretty
l**eve**l	
lib**ert**y	
libr**ary**	canary dictionary necessary secretary
lie	believe
l**ie**	die pie tie field
lied	replied
lies	flies
l**ife**	knife wife
l**ift**	drift gift

diamond lemon salmon Monday

grade trade reader

strength

develop eve fever event prevent eleventh
seventeen seventh forever whatever whenever

concert desert entertain entertainment fertile property

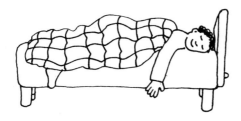

light	delight flight
light	bright delight fight flight fright might night right sight tight tonight
lightning	
lightning	
like	hike
limb	
limb	
lime	time
limit	
line	linen
line	fine mine nine shine sunshine wine engine imagine machine
linen	line
lion	million
lion	million union region
liquid	
list	listen
listen	list
listening	
listening	

delighted knight midnight mighty

dining listening shining

timber

limit

limb

equip equipment

dining lightning shining

artist blister distant district minister mistake
mistress scientist wrist

li tre	
litre	
little	
l ive	give river arrive dive drive driver five knives wives
l oad	road
loaf	
loaves	
lock	block clock o'clock
l oft	soft often
l olly	jolly
L ondon	fond pond
l onely	
lonely	
long	along belong
l ong	along belong strong among
l ook	book cook hook shook took snooker
l oose	goose choose
l orries	
lorries	
l orry	sorry worry

centimetre metre

military quality split polite

float loaves

float loaf

stone tone zone honest prisoner stationery
pioneer shone

colony nylon

horror

hurries fries

lose	close
lose	whose chose chosen close hose nose rose suppose those
loss	
loss	
lost	cost frost almost ghost most post
loud	aloud cloud
loud	aloud cloud proud
love	glove lovely
love	above glove lovely move prove drove stove
lovely	glove love
lovely	above glove love move prove drove stove
low	below blow flow slow clown
lower	slower flower
luck	bucket duck struck truck
luckily	
lumps	
lumps	
lunch	bunch
lying	dying

blossom

blossom boss moss

stuck

mumps

mumps umpire

machine	stomach
mach**ine**	fine line mine nine shine sunshine wine engine imagine
ma**chin**ery	
mach**ine**ry	
machin**ery**	
machi**ner**y	
m**ade**	blade shade spade
magaz**ine**	
magic	magician
magician	magic
m**aid**	afraid laid paid raid said
m**ail**	fail jail nail rail sail snail tail trail
m**ain**	again chain pain paint plain
major	
majority	
major**ity**	

chin

magazine miner nineteen outline pine vine
cabinet continent engineer happiness
mineral vinegar medicine

bakery celery discovery embroidery jewellery
mystery slippery stationery

energy miner mineral nervous owner partner
prisoner stationery

machinery miner nineteen outline pine vine
cabinet continent engineer happiness
mineral vinegar medicine

majority

major

community opportunity publicity quality quantity

make	bake baker brake cake lake rake shake snake take wake
making	asking baking king kingdom taking
man	manage woman many
manage	bandage cabbage cottage language message village age cage page rage stage
man age	man woman many
man ner	
manufacture	
manufact ure	
man ufacture	
many	any
man y	man manage woman
mar ble	
March	
mark	bark dark market park
mark et	bark dark mark park
married	carried
marry	carry
master	fast last past castle breakfast
match	catch watch

manufacture command fisherman gentleman human

adventure agriculture furniture future moisture nature temperature

attractive exactly subtract tract subtraction traction character

manner command fisherman gentleman human

March

marble

mate	climate material
m**ate**	ate date gate hate late plate
material	climate mate
m**atter**	chatter
M**ay**	
m**eal**	deal heal real seal health
m**ean**	clean ocean
meant	
me**an**t	
me**ant**	
meanwhile	
m**ean**while	
meanwh**ile**	
m**eas**les	
m**easure**	pleasure treasure
mea**sure**	pleasure treasure sure
m**eat**	beat beaten eat neat seat theatre great
media	
med**ia**	
medical	

pay ray stay

meanwhile

bean meanwhile

accountant distant vacant lantern advantage plantation quantity

meant

bean mean

fertile missile smile tile silence silent

peas pleased tease grease increase teaspoon

immediately

medical medicine

medicine

med ical

medic ine

med icine

medic**ine**

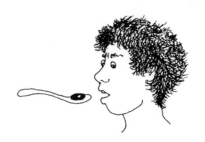

m**eet**	feet sheet street sweet teeth
m**elt**	belt felt
member	remember
memory	
m**en**	ten
m**erry**	berry cherry
mess	message
message	mess
mess**age**	bandage cabbage cottage language manage village age cage page rage stage
metal	
met al	
metal lic	
met allic	
met hod	
metre	

medicine media

medical

medical media

cabinet continent engineer happiness mineral
vinegar miner nineteen outline pine vine
machinery magazine

metallic

metallic centimetre metre geometry method sometimes

metal

metal centimetre metre geometry method sometimes

metal metallic centimetre metre geometry sometimes

centimetre

metre	
me**tre**	
m**ice**	ice-cream nice rice twice justice office officer practice police policeman
middle	
mid**night**	
m**ight**	bright delight fight flight fright light night right sight tight tonight
m**ight**y	
m**ile**	awhile pile while
milit**ary**	
mi**lit**ary	
m**ilk**	silk
m**ill**	
mill**ion**	lion
mill**ion**	union region lion
m**ind**	behind find hind kind wind
m**ine**	fine line nine shine sunshine wine engine imagine machine
miner	
mi**ner**	

centimetre metal metallic geometry method sometimes

centimetre litre

delighted knight lightning mighty

delighted knight lightning midnight

boundary February January stationary

quality split litre polite

kill pillow

mineral

energy machinery mineral nervous owner partner
prisoner stationery

miner

mineral

mineral

mineral

minister

minister

minute

mirror

mischief

mischief

miss

missed

missile

missile

mistake

mistake

nut peanut

chief handkerchief

chief handkerchief thief

hissed

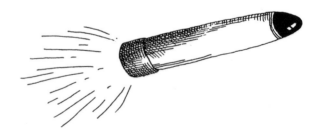

nineteen outline pine vine cabinet continent
engineer happiness mineral vinegar
machinery magazine medicine

miner

cabinet continent engineer happiness
vinegar miner nineteen outline pine vine
machinery magazine medicine

energy machinery miner nervous owner partner
prisoner stationery

blister

artist blister distant district mistake
mistress scientist wrist listening

error horror terror

missile permission

miss permission

fertile meanwhile smile tile silence silent

awake bakery

artist blister distant district minister
mistress scientist wrist listening

mister	sister
mistress	
mistress	
mix	fix six sixty
model	
modern	
moisture	
moisture	
moment	government cement
Monday	
Monday	
Monday	
money	honey
money	honey done none one alone bone telephone throne gone
monkey	donkey key
month	front
moon	noon soon spoon
more	before shore sore store
morning	born corn corner horn worn

artist blister distant district minister
mistake scientist wrist listening

expressed press progress

delicious delighted deliver

adventure agriculture furniture future manufacture nature
temperature

noise poison

Tuesday Wednesday Thursday Friday Saturday Sunday

diamond lemon lemonade salmon

condition diamond second

A B C D E F G H I J K L M N O P Q R S T U V W X Y Z

moss	
most	almost
most	almost ghost post cost frost lost
moth	
mother	grandmother
mother	another brother other bother
motion	
motion	
motive	
motive	
motor	
motor	
mould	boulder shoulder smoulder could should would
mound	around bound found ground playground pound round sound wound
mount	mountain
mount	amount count mountain
mountain	mount
mountain	amount count mount
mountain	Britain captain certain

blossom boss loss

bothers

motive motor

condition exhibition invention production

attractive expensive forgive native deliver alive

motor motion

motive motion

photo photograph

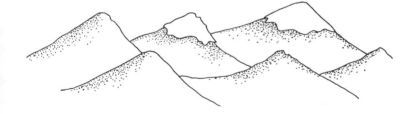

moun**tain**ous

mo**unt** ainous

mountain**ous**

mo**use** | house

mo**uth** | south

m**ove** | prove above glove love lovely drove stove

Mr | Mrs

Mr s | Mr

m**uch** | such

m**uddle** | puddle

mudd le | muddy

mudd y | muddle

multiplic**ation**

multipl ication

m**ult** iplication

multipl y

mum | mummy

mum my | mum

m**umps**

curtain fountain contain entertain entertainment obtain

account accountant fountain

dangerous jealous murderous nervous

appreciation association destination formation information irrigation multiplication occupation operation plantation recreation stationary stationery

multiply

agriculture result difficult

multiplication

lumps

m**ump**s

murder

m**urd**er

murdered

m**urd**ered

murderous

murder**ous**

m**urd**erous

murd**ero**us

m**use**

m**use**um

music

m**ust**

m**utton**

my**self**

myst**ery**

excuse use useful

dust just justice

herself himself itself self yourself

lumps umpire

murdered murderous

murdered murderous sturdy Saturday

murder murderous

murder murderous sturdy Saturday

murder murdered

dangerous jealous mountainous nervous

murder murdered sturdy Saturday

dangerous hero zero

amuse amusement fuse refuse

button

bakery celery discovery embroidery jewellery
machinery slippery stationery

nail	snail
nail	fail jail mail rail sail snail tail trail
name	game same
narrow	arrow
nation	examination national
nation	examination invitation population station national
national	examination nation
national	examination invitation nation population station
native	
native	
natural	
natural	
nature	
nature	
nature	
naughty	caught daughter taught laughter
navy	
near	clear dear ear hear year bear tear wear early earn earth heard learn heart

attractive expensive forgive motive deliver alive

nature natural

native nature

nature

natural

native natural

adventure agriculture furniture future manufacture moisture temperature

n**ear**ly	
n**eat**	beat beaten eat meat seat theatre great
necess**ary**	dictionary secretary canary library
n**eck**	
need	needle
n**eed**	feed needle seed
needle	need
n**eed**le	feed need seed
neigh	
n**eigh**	
n**eigh**bour	eight weigh weight height
neigh**our**	colour honour favourite journey flour hour our course court four pour your
neighbourhood	
neighbour**hood**	
neighbourh**ood**	
neigh**bour**hood	
neighb**our**hood	

n**eigh**bourhood	
neither	either

fear learned search wearing

---

deck speck wreck

---

neighbourhood

eighteen eighth freight neighbourhood

---

neigh

hood

goodness hood wooden

harbour labour

behaviour favour harbour labour journal fourteen fourth yours courage sour

eighteen eighth freight neigh

nerv**ous**

nervous

nervous

nest | best contest rest test west question

never | ever however every several

new | knew newspaper

new | few newspaper blew flew sew

news | newspaper

newspaper | news

news**paper** | paper

new**s**paper | knew new

newspaper | few new blew flew sew

next |

nice | ice-cream mice rice twice justice office officer practice police policeman

niece | piece

night | bright delight fight flight fright light might right sight tight tonight

nine | ninety

nine | fine line mine shine sunshine wine engine imagine machine

nine**teen**

dangerous jealous mountainous murderous

energy machinery miner mineral owner partner prisoner stationery

serve service

thirteen fourteen fifteen sixteen seventeen eighteen

nineteen

nineteen

ninety | nine

ninth

nobody | anybody body everybody somebody

noise

none | done honey money one alone bone telephone throne gone

noon | moon soon spoon

north | worth

nose | chose close hose rose suppose those chosen lose whose

note | vote wrote

nothing | anything everything something thing

notice

not ice

nought | bought brought fought ought thought drought

November

November

November

miner outline pine vine cabinet continent
engineer happiness mineral vinegar
machinery magazine medicine

complete concrete pretend

poison moisture

service advice ice iceberg price spice

knot

September December

September October December

clover overalls cove rove discovery oven
shovel improve improvement

now	know known snow
no**where**	anywhere everywhere somewhere where
nuis**ance**	
n**umber**	dumb thumb
n**urse**	purse
n**urse**	burst purse
nut	peanut minute
ny**lon**	

appearance disappearance importance instance

$$1\ 2\ 3\ 4\ 5\ 6\ 7\ 8\ 9\ 10\ 11\ 12\ 13\ 14\ 15$$

colony lonely

oak	cloak soak
oar	roar
oasis	
oats	boat coat goat throat
obey	disobey
obey	disobey grey they eye
object	
obtain	
occupation	
occupation	
occupied	
occupy	
ocean	clean mean
o'clock	block clock lock
October	
odd	
offer	office officer
office	officer
office	offer officer

boast toast

collect perfect project respect

contain entertain entertainment curtain fountain mountainous

appreciation association destination formation information irrigation multiplication operation plantation recreation stationary stationery

occupied occupy

occupation occupy

occupation occupied

September November December

office	justice officer practice ice-cream mice nice rice twice police policeman
officer	office
officer	offer office
officer	justice office practice ice-cream mice nice rice twice police policeman
often	ten tent tenth
often	loft soft
oil	boil soil spoil
ointment	
ointment	
old	cold fold gold hold sold told
once	only
one	anyone everyone someone
one	done none honey money alone bone telephone throne gone
onion	
only	once
open	pen pence pencil penny spend spent
opera	

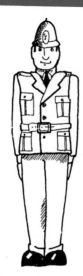

appoint appointment disappoint disappointment

agreement amusement appointment argument
development disappointment entertainment equipment
improvement instrument payment refreshment settlement
statement

operation

opera

opera

operation

operation

operation

operation

opportunity

opportunity

opportunity

opposite

orange

orchard

orchard

orchard

orchard

change danger strange

orchestra

chest

order

sword word

copper operation perfect permission proper property slippery temperature whisper

operation proper property envelope

opera

appreciation association destination formation information irrigation multiplication occupation plantation recreation stationary stationery

copper opera perfect permission proper property slippery temperature whisper

opera proper property envelope

import importance support transport

community unit unite

community majority publicity quality quantity

polite unite

porch

harden

harbour harden harness harvest chart share wharf wharves character

afterwards backwards forwards cardboard guard harden pardon regard towards

ore

organ

organise

organise

other	another brother mother bother
ought	bought brought fought nought thought drought
our	flour hour course court four pour your colour favourite honour neighbour journey
ourselves	themselves
out	outdoors outside without
out	about scout shout route
outdoors	door floor poor
outdoors	out outside without

outline

outline

outside	beside inside side
outside	out outdoors without

oven

over	cover discover government

ashore core explore fore score
therefore tore wore foreign forever

organise

organ

exercise realise

throughout trout

miner nineteen pine vine cabinet continent
engineer happiness mineral vinegar
machinery magazine medicine

discovery shovel clover overalls cove rove November
improve improvement

overalls

overalls

owe

owl

own

owner

owner

oysters

known clown down town.

clover discovery

clover cover rove November discovery oven shovel improve improvement

towel tower

slowly

energy machinery miner mineral nervous partner prisoner stationery

shown unknown

destroy voyage

pack	back black quack sack track
paddle	saddle
paddle	paddock
paddock	paddle
page	age cage rage stage bandage cabbage cottage language manage message village
paid	afraid laid maid raid said
pain	paint
pain	again chain main paint plain
paint	pain
paint	again chain main pain plain
pair	air aircraft airport chair dairy fair fairly fairy hair
palace	fireplace lace place
palace	surface face fireplace lace place race space
pale	sale tale Wales
palm	
pant	ant plant elephant giant infants want
paper	newspaper
parade	paragraph separate
paragraph	parade separate
paragraph	geography

calm salmon

parcel	parents
p**ar**don	
pardon	
parents	parcel
p**ar**k	bark dark mark market
part	apart parties party
particular	
p**ar**ticular	
particular	
parties	apart part party
partner	
p**ar**tner	
partner	
part**ner**	
party	apart part parties
pass	
p**ass**	
passenger	
p**ass**enger	
p**ast**	fast last master castle breakfast

cardboard guard harden regard afterwards backwards forwards orchard towards

particular partner prepare spare

partner

artist cart chart partner tart

pardon partner prepare spare

particular

artist cart chart particular tart

pardon particular prepare spare

energy machinery miner mineral nervous owner prisoner stationery

passenger

brass association ass passenger

pass

ass association brass pass

paste

paste

patch

patch

path | footpath

path | bath father rather gather bathe

paw | draw drawer law saw see-saw straw

pay

pay

payment

payment

peace

peach

peach

peak

peak

peanut | nut minute

pear

pear

haste taste waste fasten

haste taste waste cast fasten plastic

hatch scratch

butcher fetch hatch hitch pitch scratch stitch

payment

May ray stay

pay

agreement amusement appointment argument development disappointment entertainment equipment improvement instrument ointment refreshment settlement statement

peach peak peas pear

peace peak peas pear

preacher reaches

peace peach peas pear

weak

peace peach peak peas

appear appearance disappear disappearance spear

pea s

peas

pen	pence pencil penny spend spent open
pen ce	pen pencil penny spend spent open
pence	fence difference experience science
pencil	pen pence penny spend spent open
penny	pen pence pencil spend spent open

people

per**fect**

per fect

per**fume**	fume
per fume	perhaps person period
per haps	perfume person period
per iod	perfume perhaps person

per**miss** ion

per mission

per**son**	reason season son
per son	perfume perhaps period
pe**trol**	control

photo

peace peach peak pear

measles pleased tease grease increase teaspoon

collect object project respect

copper opera operation permission proper property
slippery temperature whisper

miss missile

copper opera operation perfect proper property
slippery temperature whisper

photograph

ph**oto**

photograph

ph**oto**graph

photo**graph**

photog**rap**h

phr**ase**

piano

p**ick**	brick kick quick stick thick trick
picnic	picture
picture	picnic
pic**ture**	capture puncture
pie	piece
p**ie**	die lie tie field
piece	pie
p**iece**	niece
p**ier**ce	
pi**ge**on	
pi**ge**on	
p**ile**	awhile mile while
p**ill**ow	
pil**low**	

photograph motor

photo

photo motor

graph telegraph

graph telegraph rapid rapidly wrap

vase

fierce

geometry

intelligent

kill mill

slowly

pilot

pimple

pinch   inch

pine

pine

pine

pink   drink think

pint

pioneer

pioneer

pipe   ripe wipe

pirate

pitch

pitch

pitch

place   fireplace lace palace

place   face fireplace lace race space
palace surface

plain   again chain main pain paint

simple

miner nineteen outline vine cabinet continent
engineer happiness mineral vinegar
machinery magazine medicine

happiness

happiness spin

print sprint

honest prisoner stationery shone lonely stone
tone zone

engineer steer

chocolate immediately private appreciate decorate skate
state statement whatever

hitch stitch

butcher fetch hatch hitch patch scratch
stitch

hospital

plan	plane plant
plane	plan plant
plant	plan plane
pl**ant**	ant pant elephant giant infants want
pl**ant**ation	
plant**ation**	
pl**ant**ation	
pl**ast**ic	
pl**ate**	late later
pl**ate**	ate date gate hate late mate
p**lay**	clay lay
player	
pl**ayer**	
playful	
play**ful**	
playg**round**	around ground round
pleasant	pleasure please
pl**ease**	disease
please	pleasant pleasure

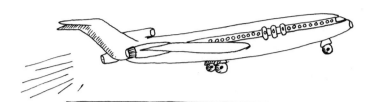

lantern

appreciation association destination formation information irrigation multiplication occupation operation recreation stationary stationery

advantage lantern accountant distant vacant quantity meant

haste paste taste waste cast fasten

playful

prayer

player

graceful handful successful thoughtful

pleased	
pleased	
pleasure	please pleasant
pleasure	measure treasure
pleasure	measure treasure sure
plenty	lent
plenty	bent lent sent spent twenty went
plough	although though enough rough tough cough
pocket	rocket
poem	
poet	
poet	
poet	
poetry	
poetry	
poetry	
point	join
poison	
poison	
polar	popular
pole	tadpole

tease grease increase

measles peas tease grease increase teaspoon

poet poetry

poetry

poem poetry

poetry hoe tomatoes

poet

poem poet

poet hoe tomatoes

prison prisoner

noise moisture

pole	hole tadpole whole
police	policeman
po**lice**	policeman justice office officer practice ice-cream mice nice rice twice
policeman	police
po**lice**man	police justice office officer practice ice-cream mice nice rice twice
po**lite**	
po**lit**e	
pond	fond London
pony	
pool	cool school stool tools wool
poor	door floor outdoors
popu**lar**	polar
popu**lation**	examination invitation nation station national
porch	
por**ridge**	bridge ridge
port	airport important report sport
position	deposit positive
positive	deposit position
possible	impossible

unite opposite

military quality split litre

stony colony

orchard

post	almost ghost most cost frost lost
post	postman
post**age**	
postman	post
pot**ato**	
pota**toes**	toes
pota**toes**	goes toes shoes does doesn't
pouch	touch
pound	around bound found ground mound playground round sound wound
pour	course court four your flour hour our journey colour honour favourite neighbour
pow der	power
pow er	powder
pract ice	practise
pract ice	act practise action
pract**ice**	justice office officer police policeman ice-cream mice nice rice twice
pract ise	practice
pract ise	act practice action
praise	raise
prais e	daisy raise waist

advantage average carriage courage damage sausage
voyage

atom atomic tomato tomatoes

A B C D E F G H I J K L M N O **P** Q R S T U V W X Y Z

pray

pray

prayer

prayer

prayer

preacher

preacher

prepare

prepare

present

absent sent sentence

press

press

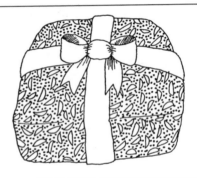

pretend

pretend

pretend

pretty

better letter lettuce

prevent

prevent

prevent

prayer

crayon ray prayer

pray

crayon pray ray

player

reaches ache

peach reaches

bare barely dare rare share spare area

spare pardon particular partner

expressed

expressed progress mistress

attend tender

attend calendar friendship independence independent
splendid tender

complete concrete nineteen

event seventeen eleventh seventh

event invent inventor vent seventeen eleventh
seventh adventure invention

event eleventh seventeen seventh forever whatever
whenever develop level eve fever

price

prince   princess

prince   since princess

princess   prince

princess   prince since

principal

principal

principle

principle

print

print

print

prison

prison

prisoner

prisoner

prisoner

prisoner

private

advice ice iceberg spice notice service

principle

principle print sprint

principal

principal print sprint

sprint

sprint pint

principal principle sprint

prisoner

poison prisoner

prison

poison prison

energy machinery miner mineral nervous owner
partner stationery

stationery honest pioneer shone lonely stone
tone zone

chocolate immediately pirate appreciate decorate skate
state statement whatever

prize	size
probably	babies baby

process

process

procession

procession

produce

produce

product

product

production

production

production

program	programme
programme	program

progress

project

promise	rise sunrise surprise wise
proof	roof

proper

procession

success successful procession

process

process success successful

product production

saucepan

production

produce production

product

produce product

condition exhibition invention motion

expressed press mistress

collect object perfect respect

property

proper

proper

proper

property

property

property

property

property

protect

correct elect electric electricity expect
insect select subject

protection

proud

aloud cloud loud

prove

move above glove love lovely drove
stove

provide

public

publicity

publicity

pudding

puddle

puddle

pudding

puddle

muddle

copper opera operation perfect permission property slippery temperature whisper

drop property

opera operation property envelope

proper

concert desert entertain entertainment fertile liberty

copper opera operation perfect permission proper slippery temperature whisper

drop proper

opera operation proper envelope

collection direction election section

aside guide stride tide consider embroidery

publicity

public

community majority opportunity quality quantity

pull	bull bulldozer full
pump	bump jump
puncture	capture picture
pupils	
puppy	
pure	
pure	
purple	purse
purpose	
purse	nurse
purse	burst nurse
purse	purple
push	bush brush rush thrush
put	but butter shut
puzzle	
pyjamas	

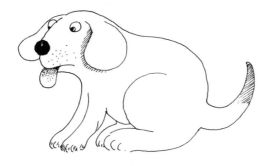

purpose

cure figure surely

pure

damage

quack	back black pack sack track
quality	
quality	
quality	
quality	
quantity	
quantity	
quantity	
quarrel	
quarter	art article smart
queen	been between green seen
queer	cheer deer
question	best contest nest rest test west
quick	brick kick pick stick thick trick
quiet	quietly
quietly	quiet
quite	bite invite kite white write
quite	fruit suit tracksuit biscuit

quantity quarrel acquainted equal

gradual gradually habitual equal

community majority opportunity publicity quantity

military split litre polite

quality quarrel acquainted equal

accountant distant vacant lantern advantage plantation meant

community majority opportunity publicity quality

quality quantity acquainted equal

rabbit	grabbed
r**ace**	face fireplace lace place space palace surface
radio	
r**aft**	
rage	garage
r**age**	age cage page stage bandage cabbage cottage language manage message village
raid	afraid
r**aid**	afraid laid maid paid said
rail	trail
r**ail**	fail jail mail nail sail snail tail trail
r**ailway**	
rail**way**	
rain	grain rainbow train
rainbow	grain rain train
raise	praise
r**aise**	daisy praise waist
rake	brake
r**ake**	bake baker brake cake lake make shake snake take wake
ramp	

aft afterwards

daily hail

highway sway

tramp

ramp

ramp

rang | bang hang sang

rapid

rapid

rapidly

rapidly

rare

rate | celebrate separate

rather | bath father path gather bathe

raw | draw drawer straw

ray

ray

reach | beach each teach teacher

reaches

reaches

read | already bread ready spread thread

reader

reader

reader

ready | already bread spread thread read

tram tramp

tramp swamp

rapidly

rapidly wrap graph photograph telegraph

rapid

rapid wrap graph photograph telegraph

bare barely dare prepare share spare area

crayon pray prayer

May pay stay

preacher ache

peach preacher

dread

grade lemonade trade

dread steady

A
B
C
D
E
F
G
H
I
J
K
L
M
N
O
P
Q
R
S
T
U
V
W
X
Y
Z

real	deal heal meal seal health
realise	
rea**lise**	
re**al**ise	
really	
reason	season
rea**son**	season person son
re**as**on	easily easy season
recei**pt**	receive
re**cei**ve	receipt
record	
record	
record	
recorder	
re**cord**er	
rec**ord**er	
recre**ation**	
re**crea**tion	
recr**eat**ion	
red	hundred

really

exercise organise

really steal jealous wealth wealthy

realise steal jealous wealth wealthy

recorder

cord recorder

afford border cord ford recorder

record

cord record

afford border cord ford record

appreciation association destination formation information irrigation multiplication occupation operation plantation stationary stationery

scream

heat treat treaty wheat

refe**ree**   three tree

refresh

re**fresh**

refreshment

re**fresh**ment

refresh**ment**

re**fuse**

ref**use**

reg**ard**

re**gard**

reg**ion**   million union lion

reign

rely

rem**ain**

re**member**   member

rem**ind**

rent

rep**lied**   lied

reply

refreshment

fresh refreshment

refresh

fresh refresh

agreement amusement appointment argument
development disappointment entertainment equipment
improvement instrument ointment payment settlement
statement

fuse

amuse amusement fuse muse

cardboard guard harden pardon afterwards backwards
forwards orchard towards

vinegar

foreign

barely entirely surely

acquainted brain explain gain sprain

blind kindness indeed index industry

current

re**port**	airport important port sport
resc**ue**	
resp**ect**	
rest	arrest interested forest
r**est**	best contest nest test west question
res**ult**	
ret**urn**	burn turn
re**ward**	war ward warm warship
ribbon	
r**ice**	ice-cream mice nice twice justice office officer practice police policeman
r**ich**	which
r**ide**	decide divide hide side slide wide
ridge	bridge porridge
ri**fle**	trifle
rift	
r**ift**	
right	bright fright (all right)
r**ight**	bright delight fight flight fright light might night sight tight tonight
ring	bring bringing during spring string
r**ipe**	pipe wipe

avenue continue due statue Tuesday value

collect object perfect project

agriculture multiplication agriculture

thrifty

fifteen swift thrifty fifth

rise	sunrise surprise
rise	sunrise surprise wise promise
river	driver
river	give live arrive dive drive driver five knives wives
road	load
roam	foam
roar	oar
roast	coast
robber	rubber
rock	rocket
rocket	rock
rocket	pocket
rode	trod
roller	
roof	proof
room	bedroom broom
rooster	
root	boot shoot foot
rope	Europe
rope	hope Europe

rose	chose close hose nose suppose those chosen lose whose
rough	through
rough	enough tough plough although though cough
round	around ground playground
round	around bound found ground mound playground pound sound wound
route	about out scout shout
rove	
row	grow grown throw thrown brown crown drown growl
rubber	robber
rugby	
rule	
ruler	
rush	brush thrush
rush	brush thrush bush push

cove clover overalls November discovery oven
shovel improve improvement

ruler

rule

A B C D E F G H I J K L M N O P Q R S T U V W X Y Z

sack	back black pack quack track
saddle	paddle
safe	safely
safely	safe
said	afraid laid maid paid raid
said	sail sailor
sail	sailor said
sail	fail jail mail nail rail snail tail trail
sailor	tailor
sailor	sail said
salad	
sale	pale tale Wales
salmon	
salmon	
salmon	
salt	altogether although
salute	
same	game name
sand	sandals thousand
sandals	sand thousand

salute salmon

---

calm palm

salad salute

diamond lemon lemonade Monday

---

salad salmon

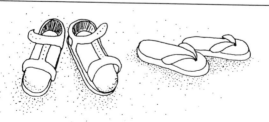

s**and**als	**bandage candle grand hand handkerchief handle standard**
s**and**wich	
s**ang**	bang hang rang
sa**tell**ite	tell
satis**factory**	factory
satisfactory	satisfy
satis**fact**ory	fact factory
satisfy	satisfactory
Satur**day**	
Satur**d**ay	
sauce	saucer
saucepan	
saucepan	
sa**uce**pan	
saucer	sauce
sausage	
sausage	
saus**age**	

s**ave**	brave cave gave have
s**aw**	draw drawer law paw see-saw straw

handful command wander

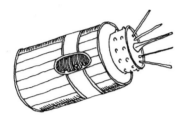

Sunday Monday Tuesday Wednesday Thursday Friday

murder murdered murderous sturdy

sausage

August author haul sausage

produce

August author haul saucepan

saucepan

advantage average carriage courage damage postage voyage

say	says
says	say
scale	
scar	
scar	
scarce	
scarce	
scare	care careful careless
scarf	
scarf	
scaring	
scaring	
scene	scenery
scenery	scene
school	cool pool stool tools wool
science	experience
science	difference experience fence pence
scientist	

whale

---

scarf scarce scaring

---

cardboard carpenter cart carve scarf caring
scarce scaring caravan

---

scaring scar scarf

---

caring scaring cardboard carpenter cart carve
scar scarf caravan

---

scar scarce scaring

---

cardboard carpenter cart carve scar caring
scarce scaring caravan

---

scarce scar scarf

---

caring scarce cardboard carpenter cart carve
scar scarf caravan

---

ancient

---

scient**ist**	
sc**iss**ors	
s**core**	
s**core**	
Scot**land**	England Ireland island land
sc**out**	about out shout route
scr**atch**	
scra**tch**	
s**cream**	
scr**een**	
sea	seal seam season seat
seal	sea seam season seat
s**eal**	deal heal meal real health
s**eam**	team
seam	sea seal season seat
s**ear**ch	
s**eason**	reason
season	sea seal seam seat
sea**son**	reason person son

302

artist blister distant district minister
mistake mistress wrist listening

kiss

core

ashore core explore fore ore
therefore tore wore forever foreign

hatch patch

butcher fetch hatch hitch patch pitch
stitch

recreation

keen

learned fear nearly wearing

season	easily easy reason
seat	beat beaten eat meat neat theatre great
seat	sea seal seam season
second	
second	
secret	secretary
secretary	secret
secretary	dictionary necessary library canary
section	
seed	seek seem seen
seed	feed need needle
seek	seed seem seen
seek	creek week
seem	seed seek seen
seen	seed seek seem
seen	been between green queen
see-saw	draw drawer law paw saw straw
seldom	
select	elect electric electricity
select	correct elect electric electricity expect insect protect subject

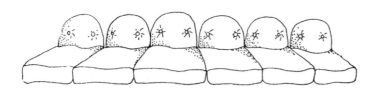

condition

diamond condition Monday

collection direction election protection

wisdom

self	herself himself itself myself yourself
send	bend friend lend spend
senior	junior
sense	
sent	sentence absent present
sent	bent lent plenty spent twenty went
sentence	sent absent present
separate	celebrate rate
separate	parade paragraph
September	
September	
September	
serious	
serve	
serve	
service	
service	
service	
set	settle upset
settle	set upset
settlement	

dense

November December

October November December

crept swept

various anxious delicious

service

nervous service

serve

nervous serve

notice advice ice iceberg price spice

settler

settle**ment**

settle**me**nt

s**ettle**ment

settler

s**ettle**r

seven

s**even**

seventeen

seven**teen**

s**even**teen

se**vent**een

s**eve**nteen

seventh

s**even**th

se**ven**th

s**eve**nth

seventy

seventy

eleven seventy even evening

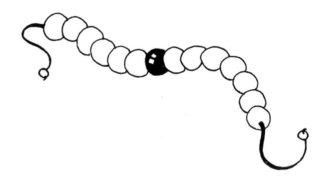

seven

agreement amusement appointment argument
development disappointment entertainment equipment
improvement instrument ointment payment refreshment
statement

agreement amusement improvement statement extremely

kettle settler

settlement

kettle settlement

seventh

thirteen fourteen fifteen sixteen eighteen nineteen

eleventh seventh event prevent

event invent inventor prevent vent eleventh
seventh adventure invention

eleventh seventh event prevent forever whatever
whenever develop level eve fever

seventeen

eleventh seventeen event prevent

eleventh event invent inventor prevent vent
seventeen adventure invention

eleventh seventeen event prevent forever whatever
whenever develop level eve fever

seventy	eleven seven even evening
several	every ever however never
sew	few new newspaper blew flew
shade	blade made spade
shake	bake baker brake cake lake make rake snake take wake
shall	hall
shall	gallon valley all call hall small allow (all right)
shape	
share	
share	
sharp	harp harpoon
shed	
sheep	deep keep steep
sheet	feet meet street sweet teeth
shelf	
shelf	
shell	jelly smell spell swell
shelter	
shelter	

ape cape gape tape

bare barely dare prepare rare spare area

harbour harden harness harvest chart orchard wharf wharves character

shelf shelter shelves shepherd

shed shelter shelves shepherd

twelfth

knelt

shed shelf shelves shepherd

she**lves**

shelves

shep**herd**

shepherd

shine   sunshine

sh**ine**   fine line mine nine sunshine wine
                            engine imagine machine

shi**ning**

ship

shi**rt**   dirt dirty thirty

sh**oe**   canoe

sh**oes**   does doesn't goes potatoes toes

sh**one**

sh**ook**   book cook hook look took snooker

sh**oot**   boot root foot

s**hop**   hope

sh**ore**   before more sore store

sh**ort**   sort

s**hot**   hot hotel

should   shoulder

wolves

shed shelf shelter shepherd

herd

shed shelf shelter shelves

dining lightning listening

honest prisoner stationery pioneer lonely stone
tone zone

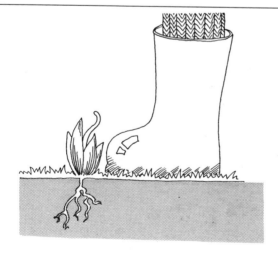

should	could would boulder mould shoulder smoulder
shoulder	should
shoulder	boulder mould smoulder could should would
shout	about out scout route
shovel	
show	anyhow how however somehow
shower	
shown	
shown	
shrink	
shut	but butter put
sickness	
sickness	
side	beside inside outside
side	decide divide hide ride slide wide
sigh	high
sight	bright delight fight flight fright light might night right tight tonight
sign	design signal
signal	design sign

discovery oven clover overalls cove rove November
improve improvement

shown

shower

owner unknown

ink sink

wicked

darkness goodness happiness harness kindness

silence	
silence	
silence	
silent	
silent	
silent	
silk	milk
silver	
simple	
since	prince princess
since	sincerely
sincerely	since
sing	
sing	
singer	finger ginger
single	
sink	
sir	
sister	mister
six	sixty
six	fix mix sixty

silent

absence independence

silent fertile meanwhile missile smile tile

silence

silence fertile meanwhile missile smile tile

excellent

pimple

single

sting

sing

ink shrink

stir

sixteen	
six**teen**	
sixth	
sixty	six
s**ix**ty	fix mix six
s**ize**	prize
sk**ate**	
skin	asking
sk**ip**	
sk**irt**	
sky	
sl**ave**	
sleep	asleep sleepy
sleepy	asleep sleep
sl**ept**	kept
slid	slide
slide	slid
sl**ide**	decide divide hide ride side wide
s**lid**ing	
slip	slippers

sixth

thirteen fourteen fifteen seventeen eighteen nineteen

sixteen

appreciate decorate state statement chocolate
immediately pirate private whatever

slip whip

thirteen

grave avenue average traveller

solid

slip	
slippers	slip
slippery	
slippery	
slow	slower
slow	below blow flow low clown
slower	slow
slower	lower flower
slowly	
slowly	
small	all call hall gallon shall valley allow (all right)
smart	art article quarter
smell	jelly shell spell swell
smile	
smoke	awoke broke spoke woke
smooth	tooth
smoulder	boulder mould shoulder could should would
snail	nail

skip whip

bakery celery discovery embroidery jewellery machinery mystery stationery

copper opera operation perfect permission proper property temperature whisper

owl

pillow

fertile meanwhile missile tile silence silent

sn**ail**	fail jail mail nail rail sail tail trail
sn**ake**	bake baker brake cake lake make rake shake take wake
sn**ook**er	cook book hook look shook took
snow	snowball snowman
s**now**	know known now
snowball	snow snowman
snow**ball**	ball football balloon
snowman	snow snowball
s**oak**	cloak oak
soak	soap
soap	soak
so**ccer**	
so**cial**	
s**ock**s	stock stockings
s**oft**	loft often
s**oil**	boil oil spoil
sold	soldier
s**old**	cold fold gold hold old told
soldier	sold
so**lid**	

commercial

sliding

some	come home
some**body**	anybody body everybody nobody
some**how**	anyhow how however show
some**one**	anyone everyone one
some**thing**	anything everything nothing thing
some**time**s	
so**met**imes	
some times	
some**where**	anywhere everywhere nowhere where
son	ton won
son	person reason season
soon	moon noon spoon
sore	before more shore store
sorrow	
sorrow	
sorry	lorry worry
sort	short
sound	around bound found ground mound playground pound round wound
soup	group
sour	

crime centimetre

centimetre metre metal metallic geometry method

geometry women

borrow

barrow borrow wheelbarrow growth

behaviour favour harbour labour neighbourhood journal
fourteen fourth yours courage

south	mouth
space	face fireplace lace place race palace surface
spade	blade made shade
spare	
spare	
speak	break steak
spear	
special	especially
speck	
speech	speed
speed	speech
spell	jelly shell smell swell
spend	bend friend lend send
spend	spent pen pence pencil penny open
spent	spend pen pence pencil penny open
spent	bent lent plenty sent twenty went
spice	
spin	
splash	
splash	

bare barely dare prepare rare share area

prepare pardon particular partner

appear appearance disappear disappearance pear

deck neck wreck

advice ice iceberg price notice service

happiness pine

flash lash

ash crash flash lash ashamed ashore

sp**lend**id

spl**end**id

sp**lit**

sp**oil**   boil oil soil

sp**oke**   awoke broke smoke woke

sp**oon**   moon noon soon

s**port**   airport important port report

sp**rain**

spr**ain**

sp**read**   already bread ready thread read

sp**ring**   bring bringing during ring string

s**print**

s**print**

spr**int**

squ**are**   are aren't

st**able**

s**tack**

st**ack**

st**age**   age cage page rage bandage cabbage
                cottage language manage message village

stairs   downstairs upstairs

calendar

attend calender friendship independence independent pretend tender

military quality litre polite

brain

acquainted brain explain gain remain

print

principal principle print

print pint

unable comfortable

attack tack

attack backwards crack jacket lack tack

st**alk**	chalk talk walk
st**amp**	camp damp lamp
stand	standard understand
standard	stand understand
st**and**ard	bandage candle grand hand handkerchief handle sandals
stand**ard**	card hard hardly yard ward
star	starch start
starch	star start
start	star starch
st**arve**	
state	
st**ate**	

statement	
state**ment**	
st**ate**ment	
stat**em**ent	
st**ation**	examination invitation nation population national

carve harvest wharves

statement

appreciate decorate skate statement chocolate immediately pirate private whatever

state

agreement amusement appointment argument development disappointment entertainment equipment improvement instrument ointment payment refreshment settlement

appreciate decorate skate state chocolate immediately pirate private whatever

agreement amusement improvement settlement extremely

st**ation**ary

station**ary**

st**ation**ery

station**ery**

station**er**y

stati**one**ry

stat**ue**

st**ay**

st**ead**y

st**eak**　　　break speak

st**eal**

steam　　　steamer

s**team**　　　steamer team

steamer　　　steam

s**team**er　　　steam team

st**eel**　　　feel wheel

st**eep**　　　deep keep sheep

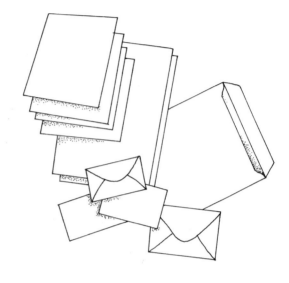

appreciation association destination formation information
irrigation multiplication occupation operation plantation
recreation stationery

boundary February January military

appreciation association destination formation information
irrigation multiplication occupation operation plantation
recreation stationary

bakery celery discovery embroidery jewellery
machinery mystery slippery

energy machinery miner mineral nervous owner
partner prisoner

prisoner honest pioneer shone lonely stone
tone zone

avenue continue due rescue Tuesday value

May pay ray

dread reader

realise really jealous wealth wealthy

st**eer**

stem

st**ick**　　　brick kick pick quick thick trick

st**iff**

st**ill**　　　fill ill will

st**ing**

st**ir**

s**tir**

st**itch**

sti**tch**

stock　　　stockings

st**ock**　　　socks stockings

stockings　　　stock

st**ock**ings　　　socks stock

st**ole**

sto**mach**　　　machine

s**tone**

st**one**

st**ony**

stood　　　stool stoop

engineer pioneer

system

cliff difficult

sing

sir

entire entirely tire

hitch pitch

butcher fetch hatch hitch patch pitch scratch

violet

tone

lonely tone zone honest prisoner stationery pioneer shone

pony colony

st**ood**	good goodbye wood food
s**tood**	stool stoop too tools tooth
stool	stoop stood
st**ool**	cool pool school tools wool
s**tool**	stoop too tools tooth stood
stoop	stool stood
s**toop**	stool too tools tooth stood
store	storm story
st**ore**	before more shore sore
storm	store story
st**orm**	form worm
story	history
story	store storm
st**ove**	drove above glove love lovely move prove
straight	strange
strange	straight
str**ange**	change danger orange
str**anger**	
st**raw**	draw drawer raw
str**aw**	draw drawer law paw saw see-saw

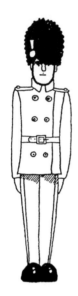

dangerous anger

A
B
C
D
E
F
G
H
I
J
K
L
M
N
O
P
Q
R
S
T
U
V
W
X
Y
Z

stream	cream dream ice-cream
street	feet meet sheet sweet teeth
strength	
strict	
stride	
strike	
string	bring bringing during ring spring
strip	stripe
strip	trip stripe
stripe	strip
stripe	strip trip
strong	along belong long among
struck	truck
struck	bucket duck luck truck
stuck	
study	
sturdy	
sturdy	
subject	correct elect electric electricity expect insect protect select
subtract	

length

district

aside guide provide tide consider embroidery

alike

luckily

murder murdered murderous Saturday

turnip

subtraction

subtr**act**

subtraction

subtr**act**ion

succ**eed**

succeed

success

success

suc**cess**

successful

successful

success**ful**

suc**cess**ful

such	much
sudden	suddenly
suddenly	sudden
su**gar**	garden garage
suit	fruit tracksuit biscuit quite
sum	summer
summer	sum
Sun**day**	

attractive exactly manufacture tract
subtraction traction character

subtract

traction attractive exactly manufacture subtract
tract character

deed indeed

success successful

successful

successful succeed

process successful procession

success

success succeed

graceful handful playful thoughtful

process success procession

Monday Tuesday Wednesday Thursday Friday Saturday

Sunday	
sung	hung hungry
sunk	
sunny	sunrise sunset
sunny	bunny funny
sunrise	rise surprise
sunrise	rise surprise wise promise
sunrise	sunny sunset
sunset	sunny sunrise
sunshine	shine
sunshine	fine line mine nine shine wine engine imagine machine
supper	upper
supper	supply support
supply	support supper
support	supply supper
support	
suppose	chose close hose nose rose those chosen lose whose
sure	measure pleasure treasure
surely	
surely	

undo

unknown

import importance transport opportunity

cure pure figure

barely entirely rely

sur**face**	face
sur**face**	palace face fireplace lace place race space
surpr**ise**	rise sunrise
surpr**ise**	rise sunrise wise promise
surr**ound**	
swam	
swam	
swamp	
sw**amp**	
swa**mp**	

swa**n**	
s**wan**	
s**way**	
swa**y**	
swee**p**	
sw**eet**	feet meet sheet street teeth
s**well**	dwell well
s**well**	jelly shell smell spell
sw**ept**	
swi**ft**	

boundary

swamp

swamp swan sway

swam

ramp tramp

swan swam sway

swamp swam sway

wander

highway railway

swam swamp swan

weekly

crept September

fifteen rift thrifty fifth

swim

swimmer

swing   wing

sword   word

sword   order word

swum

system

swimmer

swim

stem

table	vegetable
t**a**ble	able valuable vegetable
tack	
t**a**ck	
tad**pole**	pole
tadp**ole**	hole pole whole
tail	tailor
t**ail**	fail jail mail nail rail sail snail trail
tailor	tail
t**ailor**	sailor
t**ake**	bake baker brake cake lake make rake shake snake wake
ta**king**	asking backing king kingdom making
t**ale**	pale sale Wales
t**alk**	chalk stalk walk
t**ame**	
t**ape**	
tar	
target	
t**art**	
t**art**	

348

attack stack

attack backwards crack jacket lack stack

ashamed flame frame lame camera

ape cape gape shape

target tart

tar tart

tar target

artist cart chart particular partner

t**aste**	
t**ast**e	
t**aught**	caught daughter naughty laughter
t**ax**	
tea	teach teacher teaching
teach	tea teacher teaching
t**each**	beach each reach teacher
teacher	tea teach teaching
t**each**er	beach each reach teach
teaching	tea teach teacher
team	steam steamer
t**eam**	seam
t**ear**	bear wear clear dear ear hear near year early earn earth heard learn heart
t**ease**	
t**eas**e	
tease	
t**eas**poon	
teaspoon	
t**eet**h	feet meet sheet street sweet
telegram	

haste paste waste fasten

haste paste waste cast fasten plastic

axe

pleased grease increase

measles peas pleased grease increase teaspoon

teaspoon

grease increase measles peas pleased tease

tease

telegraph

teleg ram

tele gram

tele graph

tele**graph**

teleg raph

tele graph

tele**grap**h

telephone	alone bone throne done none honey money one gone
telephone	television
television	telephone
tele**vision**	division
tell	satellite

tempera**ture**

temp**er**ature

ten	tent tenth often
ten	men

tender

tender

tennis

telegraph legal

telegraph election eleventh celery

telegram

graph photograph

telegram legal

telegram election eleventh celery

graph photograph rapid rapidly wrap

adventure agriculture furniture future manufacture moisture nature

copper opera operation perfect permission proper property slippery whisper

attend pretend

attend calender friendship independence independent pretend splendid

tent	ten tenth often
tent	attention
tenth	ten tent often
term	germ
terrible	terrified terrify
terrified	terrible terrify
terrify	terrible terrified
terror	
terror	
test	contest
test	best contest nest rest west question
than	thank thankful
thank	thankful than
thankful	thank than
thankful	awful beautiful careful cheerful wonderful
that	chat hat what
the	them then these their there they
theatre	centre
theatre	beat beaten eat meat neat seat great
theft	left

error

error horror mirror

their	there the them then these they
them	themselves
them	then the their there these they
themselves	them
themselves	ourselves
then	hen when
then	them the their there these they
t**here**	where here
th**ere**	where here were
there	their the them then these they
there**fore**	
theref**ore**	
therefore.	
these	the them then their there they
they	the them then their there these
th**ey**	disobey grey obey eye
th**ick**	brick kick pick quick stick trick
th**icken**	chicken
th**ief**	chief handkerchief mischief
th**ieves**	

fore forever foreign

ashore core explore fore ore score
tore wore foreign forever

breathe bothers feather further

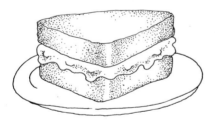

achieve

thin	thing think
thing	think thin
thing	anything everything nothing something
think	thing thin
think	drink pink
third	bird
thirst	first
thirteen	
thirteen	
thirty	dirt dirty shirt
this	his history whistle
thorn	
those	chose hose chosen whose
those	chose close hose nose rose suppose chosen lose whose
though	although enough rough tough cough plough
thought	bought brought fought nought ought drought
thoughtful	
thoughtful	
thousand	sand sandals

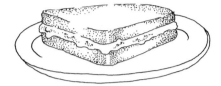

fourteen fifteen sixteen seventeen eighteen nineteen

skirt

torn

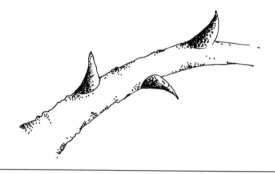

throughout bough

graceful handful playful successful

th **read**	already bread ready spread read
th **ree**	referee tree
th **rew**	drew grew
th **rifty**	
thr **ifty**	
thr **oat**	boat coat goat oats
thr **one**	alone bone telephone gone one done none honey money
thr **ottle**	bottle
thr **ottle**	bottle bottom
th **rough**	rough
thr **oughout**	
through **out**	
th **row**	grow grown row thrown brown crown drown growl
th **rown**	grown brown crown drown
th **rown**	grow grown row throw brown crown drown growl
th **rush**	brush rush
thr **ush**	brush rush bush push
th **umb**	dumb number
th **under**	under understand

rift

fifteen rift swift fifth

thoughtful bough

outline trout

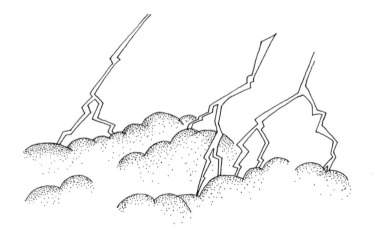

Thurs**day**	
ticket	cricket wicket
tide	
tie	die lie pie field
tiger	
tight	bright delight fight flight fright light might night right sight tonight
tile	
tile	
timber	
time	lime
tin	tiny
tiny	tin
tire	
tire	
tire	
tired	hired
toast	
toast	
tobacco	toboggan
toboggan	tobacco

Friday Saturday Sunday Monday Tuesday Wednesday

aside guide provide stride consider embroidery

fertile

fertile meanwhile missile smile silence silent

limb

entire entirely

entire entirely stir

entire entirely umpire direction

boast

boast oasis

A B C D E F G H I J K L M N O P Q R S T U V W X Y Z

to**day**	day holiday
today	together tomorrow tonight
toes	potatoes
t**oes**	goes potatoes shoes does doesn't
t**offee**	coffee
together	altogether
tog**ether**	altogether whether
together	today tomorrow tonight
t**old**	cold fold gold hold old sold
tomato	
tom**ato**	
tomatoes	
tom**ato**es	
tomat**oe**s	
tomorrow	today together tonight
ton	son won
tone	
t**one**	
ton**gue**	
t**ong**ue	

364

tomatoes

tomatoes atom atomic potato

tomato

tomato atom atomic potato

hoe poet poetry

stone

lonely stone zone honest prisoner stationery
pioneer shone

league argue

wrong

to night	today together tomorrow
tonight	bright delight fight flight fright light might night right sight tight
too	stool stoop tools tooth stood
too	zoo
took	book cook hook look shook snooker
too ls	stool stoop too tooth stood
tool s	cool pool school stool wool
too th	stool stoop too tools stood
tooth	smooth
tore	
torn	
touch	pouch
tough	enough rough although though cough plough
towards	
toward s	
tow ards	
tow el	
towel	
tow er	

ashore core explore fore ore score
therefore wore foreign forever

thorn

afterwards backwards forwards

afterwards backwards forwards orchard cardboard guard
harden pardon regard

towel tower

tower towards

tower owe

towel towards

tower	
town	clown down known own
toy	boy cowboy enjoy joy
track	tracksuit
track	back black pack quack sack
tracksuit	track
tracksuit	fruit suit biscuit quite
tract	
traction	
tractor	doctor editor visitor
trade	
traffic	
trail	rail
trail	fail jail mail nail rail sail snail tail
train	grain rain rainbow
tram	
tram	
tramp	
tramp	

towel owe

attractive exactly manufacture subtract subtraction traction character

subtraction attractive exactly manufacture subtract tract character

grade lemonade reader

tramp

ramp tramp

tram

ramp

t ramp	
tr amp	
trans port	
trap	trapeze
trapeze	trap
t ravel	gravel
traveller	
tr aveller	
tr easure	measure pleasure
trea sure	measure pleasure sure
treat	
tr eat	
treaty	
tr eaty	
t ree	referee three
tribe	
tr ick	brick kick pick quick stick thick
tri cycle	bicycle cycle
t ried	cried dried
t ries	cries dries
t rifle	rifle

ramp tram

ramp swamp

import importance support opportunity

excellent jewellery cell intelligent umbrella

avenue average grave slave

treaty

heat treaty wheat recreation

treat

heat treat wheat recreation

trimmed	
trip	strip stripe
trod	rode
trouble	double
trousers	
trout	
truck	struck
truck	bucket duck luck struck
true	blue glue
trunk	drunk
trust	
trust	
truth	
try	cry dry
tube	
Tuesday	
Tuesday	
tune	
tunnel	funnel
turn	burn return
turnip	

household

outline throughout

crust

crust chorus

cube

Wednesday Thursday Friday Saturday Sunday Monday

avenue continue due rescue statue value

sturdy

tw**elf**th	
twelve	twenty
twentieth	
t**wen**ty	went
twenty	twelve
tw**ent**y	bent lent plenty sent spent went
tw**ice**	ice-cream mice nice rice justice office officer practice police policeman
t**win**s	win winter
two	
type	typewriter
typewriter	type
type**writer**	write
tyre	

shelf

ugly

umbrella

umbrella

umpire

umpire

unable

uncle

under   thunder understand
_____

under**neath**

under**neath**

under**stand**   stand standard
_____

understand   thunder under
_____

undo

un**done**   done
_____

un**happy**

un**ion**   million region lion
_____

unit

unite

un**ite**

unkn**own**

376

crumb

cell intelligent excellent traveller jewellery

entire entirely tire direction

lumps mumps

stable comfortable

beneath

beneath wreath breathe breath death feather

Sunday

happily happiness

community opportunity unite

community opportunity unit

polite opposite

owner shown

unknown

unless | less lesson

until | hunt

u**pon**

upper | supper

up**set** | set settle

up**stairs** | downstairs stairs

use | excuse useful museum

useful | excuse use museum

usual | usually

usually | usual

sunk

weapon

vac**ant**

v**alley** | gallon shall all call hall small
allow (all right)

valu**able** | vegetable able table

val**ue**

van

variety

various

various

varn**ish**

varnish

v**ase**

vege**table** | table

veget**able** | valuable able table

vent

verse

very | every

view

vill**age** | bandage cabbage cottage language manage
message age cage page rage stage

vine

accountant distant lantern advantage plantation quantity meant

avenue continue due rescue statue Tuesday

caravan advantage

various varnish

serious anxious delicious

variety varnish

fisherman foolish furnish goldfish

variety various

phrase

event invent inventor prevent seventeen eleventh seventh adventure invention

vinegar

vine

vinegar

vine**gar**

vine gar

violet

vio**let**

vio**le**t

violin

visit

visitor

visi**tor**

visitor
visit
doctor editor tractor

voice

choice

vote

note wrote

voy**age**

v**oy**age

miner nineteen outline pine cabinet continent
engineer happiness mineral vinegar
machinery magazine medicine

vine

regard

cabinet continent engineer happiness
mineral miner nineteen outline pine vine
machinery magazine medicine

violin

booklet complete

stole

violet

advantage average carriage courage damage postage
sausage

destroy oysters

waist	daisy praise raise
wait	bait
wake	bake baker brake cake lake make rake shake snake take
Wales	pale sale tale
walk	chalk stalk talk
wander	
wander	
want	ant pant plant elephant giant infants
war	reward ward warm warship
war	far farther jar
ward	reward war warm warship
ward	card hard hardly yard standard
warm	reward war ward warship
warm	alarm arm army farm farmer harm
warship	reward war ward warm
was	wasn't wash
was	wasn't has hasn't gas
wash	was wasn't
wasn't	was wash
wasn't	was has hasn't gas

command handful sandwich

swan

waste	
waste	
watch	catch match
water	later
weak	
wealth	
wealth	
wealthy	
wealthy	
weapon	
weapon	
wear	bear tear clear dear ear hear near year early earn earth heard learn heart
wearing	
weather	leather
weave	
Wednesday	
week	creek seek
weekly	
weigh	eight neighbour weight height
weight	eight eighty height

haste paste taste fasten

haste paste taste cast fasten plastic

peak

wealthy

jealous wealthy realise really steal

wealth

jealous wealth realise really steal

heap cheap

upon

fear nearly learned search

eave heave heaven

Thursday Friday Saturday Sunday Monday Tuesday

sweep

w**eigh**t	eight neighbour weigh height
wel**come**	become come
well	dwell swell
we'll	we're
went	twenty
w**ent**	bent lent plenty sent spent twenty
w**ere**	here there where
we're	we'll
west	western
w**est**	best contest nest rest test question
western	west
wh**ale**	
wharf	
w**harf**	
wharves	
w**har**ves	
wh**arve**s	
w**hat**	chat hat that
what**ever**	

scale

wharves

wharves harbour harden harness harvest chart orchard share character

wharf

wharf harbour harden harness harvest chart orchard share character

carve harvest starve

forever whenever fever

what**eve**r

wh**ate**ver

wh**eat**

wh**eat**

wh**eel**   feel steel

wheel**barrow**

w**heel**barrow

wh**eel**barrow

wheelba**rrow**

w**hen**   hen then

when**ever**

when**eve**r

when**e**ver

wh**ere**   there were here

w**here**   there here

where   anywhere everywhere nowhere somewhere

wh**ether**   altogether together

wh**ich**   rich

wh**ile**   awhile

forever whenever eleventh seventeen seventh event
prevent develop level eve fever

appreciate decorate skate state statement
chocolate immediately pirate private

heat

heat treat treaty recreation

barrow

heel

heel kneel

barrow borrow sorrow growth

forever whatever fever

forever whatever eleventh seventeen seventh
event prevent develop level eve fever

beneath enemy energy

wh**ile**	awhile mile pile
wh**ip**	
wh**irl**	girl
whis**per**	
w**his**tle	his history this
wh**ite**	bite invite kite quite write
who	whose whole
w**hole**	hole
whole	who whose
wh**ole**	hole pole tadpole
whose	who whole
w**hose**	chose hose those chosen
wh**ose**	lose chose close hose nose rose suppose those chosen
why	
w**ick**ed	
w**icket**	cricket ticket
w**ide**	decide divide hide ride side slide
widow	
width	
w**ife**	knife life

skip slip

copper opera operation perfect permission proper
property slippery temperature

sickness

width

widow

w ild	child children
w ill	fill ill still
win	twins winter
wind	window
w ind	behind find hind kind mind
window	wind
w ine	fine line mine nine shine sunshine engine imagine machine
wing	swing
w inner	dinner
winter	twins win
w ipe	pipe ripe
w ire	fire
wisdom	
w ise	rise sunrise surprise promise
w ish	British dish finish fish Irish
w itch	ditch
with	within without
within	with without
without	with within
without	out outdoors outside

seldom

wives	arrive dive drive driver five knives give live river
woke	awoke
woke	awoke broke smoke spoke
wolf	
wolves	
woman	man manage many
women	
won	wonder wonderful won't
won	son ton
wonder	won wonderful won't
wonderful	won wonder won't
wonderful	awful beautiful careful cheerful thankful
won't	don't
won't	won wonder wonderful
wood	good goodbye stood food
wooden	
wooden	
wool	cool pool school stool tools
woollen	
word	sword

golf

shelves

geometry sometimes

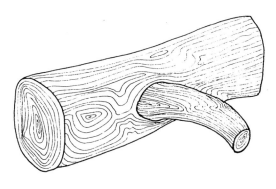

goodness hood neighbourhood

golden harden

fool foolish

w ord	order sword
word	work world worm worse worst worth worn
w ore	
w ork	fork
work	word world worm worse worst worth worn
world	word work worm worse worst worth worn
w orm	form storm
worm	word work world worse worst worth worn
w orn	born corn corner horn morning
worn	word work world worm worse worst worth
w orry	lorry sorry
w orse	horse
worse	word work world worm worst worth worn
worst	word work world worm worse worth worn
w orth	north
worth	word work world worm worse worst worn
w ould	could should boulder mould shoulder smoulder
w ound	around bound found ground mound playground pound round sound

ashore core explore fore ore score
therefore tore foreign forever

wrap

wreath

wreath

wreck

wrist

write   bite invite kite quite white

write   typewriter

wrong

wrote   note vote

rapid rapidly graph photograph telegraph

beneath underneath breathe breath death feather

breath breathe

deck neck speck

artist blister distant district minister mistake mistress scientist listening

tongue

y**ard**	c**ard** h**ard** h**ard**ly st**and**ard w**ard**
y**awn**	d**awn** l**awn**
y**ear**	cl**ear** d**ear** **ear** h**ear** n**ear** b**ear** t**ear** w**ear** **ear**ly **ear**n **ear**th h**ear**d l**ear**n h**ear**t
yell	**yell**ow
yellow	**yell**
y**ellow**	f**ellow**
yes	**yes**terday
yesterday	**yes**
y**olk**	
y**our**	c**our**se c**our**t f**our** p**our** col**our** fav**our**ite hon**our** neighb**our** j**our**ney fl**our** h**our** **our**
y**our**s	
your**self**	her**self** him**self** it**self** my**self** **self**
z**ero**	
z**one**	
z**oo**	t**oo**

folk

fourteen fourth behaviour favour harbour labour
neighbourhood journal courage sour

hero dangerous murderous

lonely stone tone honest prisoner stationery
pioneer shone